How to Run a Dog Business

Putting Your Career Where Your Heart Is

Veronica Boutelle

Dogwise™ Publishing
Wenatchee, Washington U.S.A.

How to Run a Dog Business
Putting Your Career Where Your Heart Is
Veronica Boutelle

Dogwise Publishing
A Division of Direct Book Service, Inc.
701B Poplar Wenatchee, Washington 98807
1-509-663-9115, 1-800-776-2665
www.dogwisepublishing.com / info@dogwisepublishing.com
© 2008 Veronica Boutelle

Graphic Design: Nathan Woodward
Indexing: Cheryl Smith
Cover Photo: Jennifer Murray   MPhotography   www.mphotography.com

Limits of Liability and Disclaimer of Warranty:
The author and publisher shall not be liable in the event of incidental or consequential damages in connection with, or arising out of, the furnishing, performance, or use of the instructions and suggestions contained in this book.

Library of Congress Cataloging-in-Publication Data
Boutelle, Veronica.
  How to run a dog business : putting your career where your heart is / Veronica Boutelle.
     p. cm.
  Includes index.
  ISBN-13: 978-1-929242-47-4 (alk. paper)
  1. Dog trainers. 2. Small business--Management. 3. New business enterprises--Management. I. Title.
  SF431.B68 2007
  636.7068--dc22
                                        2007032299
ISBN: 978-1-929242-47-4
Printed in the U.S.A.

TABLE OF CONTENTS

Foreword v

Introduction viii

Chapter One
New Pups: Getting Started 1

Chapter Two
Finances and Systems for Your Business............................ 6

Chapter Three
Legalities and Liabilities 10

Chapter Four
Build It and They Will Come? You Need a Marketing Plan!......... 22

Chapter Five
Keep Them Coming Back 39

Chapter Six
The Nuts and Bolts: Services, Rates, and Policies 43

Chapter Seven
Old Dogs: Growing Pains... 60

Chapter Eight
Feeling the Burn: Avoiding Professional Burnout 74

Chapter Nine
Parting Shots: A Few Extra Pieces of Advice 88

Resources 90

Acknowledgments... 118

Author Biography... 118

Index 119

I dedicate this book to my clients. Your courageous decision to pursue your dreams is why I do what I do.

Foreword

Helping the Helper

As Director of the San Francisco SPCA Academy for Dog Trainers, I had the opportunity to see Veronica in action when she ran the behavior and training department at the SF-SPCA. She said that what she most liked about the dog training world was helping other trainers to do their jobs. She mused about doing exactly that full-time, and the result was dogTEC, her consulting and seminar business, and now this book, *How to Run a Dog Business*. Veronica loves and respects dog trainers and genuinely loves helping them. And, aside from the invaluable practicalities, counsel, structure, and support she provides, there is her real-time model of how to handle clients, in this case the client being the trainer: authentically, with respect, patience and empathy. Not to mention the model of finding the niche that you like and are good at. A common theme of hers is playing to strengths and using solid strategies to handle everything else.

There was a Monday some months ago when I awoke to 86 emails in my in-box, all but five of which fell into two categories: junk and "HELP!" The triage strategy I used to sort through the mayhem was pure Veronica. The fact that I had a triage strategy and that turning to it came immediately, without agony, was pure Veronica. I could almost hear her voice in my head: "Well, of course you can't do all of them. So let's talk about how much time on a typical day you want to put into answering cold, pro-bono, distance consult requests." (They have a category!) "Once we have that time, we can work backwards and prioritize. Then we'll think about how, on a particularly bad day, you'll raise the bar and end up deleting or referring more." A plan. A conscious plan. No, wait, better—a system. First delete the junk, then delete or refer requests from people you don't know, leaving colleagues and former students. Then the bad day clause kicks in, so delete or refer anything less concise than a few lines, leaving a manageable handful. Divide these into the time available and, voila, a time allocation for each. Reply and then get on with the rest of the bad—time-wise bad—day. With some actual energy.

I also often get flashes of Veronica when I am in the offices of mental health professionals (which I have been known to be seen in). Two instances spring to mind. In one, a psychologist sagely and simply observed that I had difficulty setting limits. There are options in the face of such observations. There's the Teflon option, such as the dismissive "duh" or the "that's just who I am" or, Teflon with a side of solipsism, "somebody has to…(save the world, the world being, of course, the dogs, all of them)." There's the externalizing option, inevitably some variation on "how do I get them to stop…(inviting me, and only me apparently, to save the world, i.e., all the dogs)." The best option is, of course, the Veronica Option: absorption and reflection. "Let's think about this," she'd say and then help you think about it, always in a useful, non-stewy way. Everyone should be so lucky as to have a Veronica Option when these mental forks in the road appear. I hope that readers of this book will choose absorb-reflect a lot. Several times per page actually. If you do this, you'll end up with a tidy stable of Veronica Options.

The second Veronica flash came about when my curiosity got the better of me and I one day asked a psychiatrist who seemed to genuinely enjoy and be engaged by what she was doing, how she could stand to be a repository for people's angst and suffering all day long. She paused only briefly before saying, "I like my patients." It probably shouldn't have, but it blindsided me. The same theme has been oft-mused by my friend and colleague, Janis Bradley, whose bare reply to students and fellow trainers, when they lament the difficulties inherent in counseling dog guardians is: "you gotta find a way to like your clients." The clients being the humans, not the dogs. As Veronica so aptly points out in the book you're about to read, dog training pulls people who have great, great affinity for dogs. By happenstance, some may also have a liking of, gift for, or training in helping people. But too often, in the dog trainer's drama, the client is the perpetrator, the dog the victim and the dog trainer the tormented superhero. Burn-out city that plot is.

In helping professions, wherein this role is more frankly acknowledged than in dog training, helping the helper is a long-standing theme. Support and replenishment for those who deal with humans in need is also a hot topic in domestic situations—caring for elderly or ill parents, nurturing a special needs child, sticking by a spouse through thick. It is gratifying indeed to see the complexity and helping aspects of dog training acknowledged, taken apart, and made manageable. It will pull good people into the field and retain many more who might have otherwise burned out. I can honestly think of no better way to save all the dogs.

Jean Donaldson, author of *Culture Clash*, *Fight!*, *Mine!*, and *Dogs Are From Neptune*

August, 2007

INTRODUCTION

Is It Right For You?

Some dream of it from childhood—working with dogs for a living. I remember gathering all my stuffed dogs onto a large blanket and pretending to go down a river on our "raft," encountering all manner of adventures along the way. Or piling the plush pooches into my wagon and then walking down the street for the mail, stopping now and then for a quick training lesson. If someone had asked me at 5 years of age what I wanted to be when I grew up, I'd have said I wanted to be an animal teacher. As it turned out, I became a teacher, but of humans. It wasn't until I began to cast around for a second career that I stumbled into dog training.

Most dog trainers, walkers, and sitters come to the profession as a second career. Nearly everyone engaged in a dog business has a deep love of animals, and when this becomes combined with a high degree of frustration with (or aversion to!) traditional jobs, the lure of working with dogs full-time becomes strong. Unfortunately for those who wish to work with dogs—as trainers, walkers, sitters, or daycare providers—the choices are slim. There are few jobs available and most rarely pay much above minimum wage. Almost never do they come with health or other benefits. So for all but a few of us, to earn a living as a provider of professional dog services means starting our own businesses.

You, yourself, and you—the role of personality

Before you start your business or dive deeper into financial and legal commitments with an existing one, take a few moments to consider whether you are truly heading in a direction that is right for you.

It's easy to glamorize the benefits of being one's own boss—the flexible scheduling, being able to do things the way you see fit, being in control of your own destiny. When a business is running well, all of this is true. But the downsides are equally important—there's no one to write your monthly paycheck, no set hours and accountability to make sure the unexciting but necessary administrative tasks are completed, and the business's success or failure rests on your shoulders. Many people find working for themselves more of a challenge than anticipated, and it seems that some personalities are better suited to the life of a small business owner than others.

The first self-assessment you need to make is how comfortable you are taking risks. Many new business owners have to dip into their savings or borrow money—what if you have to? Does the mere thought of that give you the heebie-jeebies? Starting a dog training business takes less capital than most enterprises, but you still run the risk of losing money and possibly failing. It takes tenacity and perspective to face such prospects and still work hard and enthusiastically. I've seen many dog pros quit or go back to part-time work long before their businesses could reasonably be expected to succeed.

The second self-assessment has to do with your ability to problem solve and your level of self-discipline. You will face challenges and problems throughout your business career. While you don't have to enjoy solving problems, you need to be willing to tackle them head on and not sweep them under the rug. You also need to be self-disciplined, especially about those parts of the business above and beyond dealing with dogs such as marketing, bookkeeping, and following up with clients. Can you handle a variety of tasks? Do you stick with your plans over time? Could you see yourself doing this in five years? If you've answered yes to most of these questions, self-employment could be perfect for you.

You know you want to work with dogs. Now the challenge is to learn to run a company. If you're already in business for yourself, you've probably experienced some of the frustrations and pitfalls, not the least of which is waking up to realize that your business is running you, rather than the other way around. This common phenomenon can sneak up on you easily, a combination of early systems failing under the weight of increased business, of initial decisions that made perfect sense at the beginning coming back to haunt you as the business grew, and the press of day to day activities robbing your attention from the big picture needs of your enterprise. If you're already knee deep in these stressors, this book can help you dig out and create a fresh start. And if you're just getting started, the aim is to help you start off in control and stay there.

Reality check—do you really get paid to play with dogs all day?

Unfortunately not. Hands-on dog time varies by profession and business type, but all dog businesses entail more than working with dogs. As you'll see, a large portion of your time will be spent marketing your business (which isn't as frightening or awful as it sounds). Then there's the administrative time spent answering and returning phone calls and emails, handling client paperwork, and taking care of general tasks like bookkeeping. And don't underestimate the driving. Most sitters, walkers, and trainers spend a good deal of time in their cars. Another consideration for trainers is the realization early on that in most cases training owners, not dogs, is the primary task.

These are all important facts to face as you decide if a career as a dog pro is right for you. Even so, life with the dogs is a hard living to beat. If you agree, this book is for you.

A Word on the Businesses Covered in This Book

Though groomers, veterinary clinics, and other pet care providers are likely to find many of the basic concepts and ideas in this book useful, and while some of the advice given in these pages is true for any business, the book is intentionally and specifically designed for the needs, challenges, and success of dog trainers, dog walkers, pet sitters, and daycare operators.

Chapter 1

NEW PUPS: GETTING STARTED

Before committing money and time to a new career—and before you leave your day job—I suggest you find ways to experience your chosen field firsthand to make sure it is right for you. Many dog lovers attend a dog training program or start a business only to find that they don't enjoy the day-to-day routines of the job, despite an enduring love of dogs.

Volunteer

If you haven't spent a lot of time with different types of dogs or dogs in groups, try volunteering at places where dogs congregate, such as a local shelter or daycare. Some people are surprised to find that they don't enjoy the company of all dogs nearly as much as they do their family pooch.

Volunteering with a dog pro is another excellent way to get an insider's view of the career you are considering. If you are interested in training, offer to assist in a local trainer's classes. Would-be dog walkers can try to find a local walker who might welcome your company on a walk or two. Thinking of pet sitting or boarding? Ask a professional sitter if you can ride along.

Be careful to choose someone who is reputable and has credentials and experience. Then let them know you are interested in the profession and would like to offer your assistance in return for some experience. Buy them lunch or coffee to talk it over if they have time. If you are professional in your manner and sincere in your attitude (and gratitude) they'll likely be glad for the help.

Go to school

Going to school is a relatively recent option for would-be dog trainers, but already there are a profusion of dog training programs to choose from. Although you can still legally declare yourself a dog trainer without any formal education, this is becoming less acceptable as the industry professionalizes. Consider this to your advantage—you will be much more successful and help more people and dogs if you learn the trade. And, though you may have grown up with and loved dogs all your life, don't cheat yourself by falling into the "I'm really good with dogs" trap. There is a high degree of skill and knowledge involved in training, and it is too fascinating to miss out on—the study of canine body language, how dogs think and learn, the science behind behavior modification, the effects of nature and nurture on behavior—and the list goes on and on. Yes, there is a certain amount of just "being good with dogs" involved with being a good trainer. And yes, there is craft to dog training. But the craft without the science is limited and often leads to misinterpretations of dog behavior, which lead to training choices that can be inefficient and even dangerous.

Traditionally, dog trainers have been self taught, but this is changing rapidly. Dr. Ian Dunbar founded the Association of Pet Dog Trainers (APDT) in 1993 hoping to bring quality education and scientific standards to a profession that had long relied solely on mentorship, apprenticeship, or simply "being good with dogs." The impact of Dunbar and the APDT has been profound, particularly in the area of trainer certification. Schools for dog trainers have sprouted all over the country, science based training has revolutionized the field, and clients are increasingly demanding to work with trainers who have formal education and training. An unfortunate side effect of this overwhelmingly positive development is the inception of many less-than-reputable programs for dog trainers; some of which do more harm than good by spreading old misconceptions and harmful practices, others that simply take your money and teach you very little. But we also see dog training slowly becoming recognized as a skilled profession and a number of strong programs gaining ground and educating greater numbers of trainers. Dog trainers who graduate from such places are changing dog training from an anecdotally based approach to a science-based approach, and the profession, dog owners, and dogs are all the better for it.

Being well trained, so to speak, can only be to your benefit, and what's more, it is the professionally responsible thing to do, and it reduces your liability risk. If you decide to commit to the concept of education, and I strongly recommend that you do, the next step is to find the right program for you, and here, you cannot be too thorough or discriminating. There are many schools out there, but as I've mentioned, they vary greatly in content, approach to training, and quality. As you search for schools, keep these considerations in mind:

• Who are the instructors? What are their qualifications?

• What approach are they taking to dog training? Are their methods scientifically sound and humane? Are they in keeping with recent research?

• You'll see a lot of buzzwords. Some you want to see include: positive reinforcement, operant and classical conditioning, scientific method. Some to be wary of include: leadership, dominance, eclectic, and inclusive. Also, avoid anyone who promises immediate and dramatic results.

• To be ready to take clients, you need a good balance of theory and practice. Online or other remote courses can be fantastic additions to a direct education, but cannot serve as a replacement for a hands-on program and experience.

Education and training programs for walkers and sitters are definitely scarcer. There is only one training and certification program for dog walkers, the dogTEC Dog Walking Academy. Given that it would be inappropriate to toot that horn too much here, I'll just say that there's further information at the back of the book should you be interested in learning more. Pet sitters can join the National Association of Professional Pet Sitters (NAPPS) and/or Pet Sitters International (PSI) and attend their yearly conferences. PSI also has an accreditation program for pet sitters.

I strongly recommend that daycare owners have as much dog training education as possible—it will greatly increase your enjoyment of the work and the safety of yourself, others, and the dogs. Some ways to get more information:

• Join some reputable chat groups, such as APDT, Clicker Solutions, Peaceable Paws, or http://google.com/Top/Recreation/Pets/Sitters_and_Walkers

- See the Resources section at the back of this book for a list of respected dog training schools and walking and sitting certification programs.

- Read professional dog training books to familiarize yourself with some of the terminology and concepts. There's a good starter list for you in the Resources section.

Read

While not a substitute for hands-on experience, reading is key to mastering the theory behind training, and it will make you a better trainer, walker, sitter, or daycare operator. Similar to schools, all books and authors are not the same, so use the guidelines for finding a training program to help you build your library. For a list of must-reads, and how to get them, see the Resources at the back of this book.

Finding an older dog: How to find and keep a mentor

Connecting with a strong, knowledgeable mentor can make a great difference at the beginning and throughout your career. You want someone who is good at what they do, and adept at talking about it; someone who is willing to take the time to work with you and answer your questions because they care about the profession and recognize that being a mentor pushes them further, too. In short, you want a good teacher, confidant, and colleague.

To find your mentor, make a list of the various people in your area who offer the services you want to learn. Contact each person and introduce yourself. Tell them you're interested in entering the profession and ask if they would be willing to chat with you for a few moments. If you enjoy the conversation, offer to take them to lunch to continue it. Such conversations give you a chance to make a connection and build an early sense of the person's approach and professionalism. If things are going well, offer to assist them. From there you can begin to build a mentoring relationship.

For a mentor-protégé relationship to work in the long term it is important that the mentor benefits, too. Don't be afraid to ask what you can do to help your mentor, but also take initiative where appropriate. You'll have a lot of questions—be mindful of when you ask them (i.e., not during consults and training sessions), and how many you fire off in a single sitting. A good mentor will spend time on your education, but don't ask for too much. Try keeping a small notebook to jot down your questions, and then prioritize so that you get the most pressing ones answered. Consider arranging a specific time for your questions, such as after a class for trainers or during car rides for walkers and sitters.

Schools and seminars: The importance of continuing education

Your education shouldn't end after you become certified. By the time you are certified you will have realized how much there still is to know, and ongoing research and the constant refinement of methods make continuing education exciting and necessary for staying up to date.

Seminars are a great way to keep up on your education, and to meet and network with colleagues. As not all seminars and speakers share the same quality, choose with care how you spend your time and money. Once there try not to be charmed by the speaker. Instead, ask hard questions. What evidence do they have for their assertions? How does what they're saying compare with what you've read and learned previously? What is the scientific basis for their concepts?

You can find seminars and educational conferences by joining local mailing groups and keeping an eye on the APDT, IAABC, and other professional websites. See the Resources section at the end of the book for additional information.

Keep learning in between seminars. Dogwise is a fantastic source of dog related books and videos. Join their mailing list and they'll keep you up to date on all the new titles. And Tawzer Dog Videos specializes in taping seminars across the country and making them available to folks not lucky enough to be there in person. These resources are available at the back of the book.

Chapter 2

FINANCES AND SYSTEMS FOR YOUR BUSINESS

A question I'm frequently asked, and with good reason, is whether or not you can actually make a living working with dogs. The short answer is yes. But most people want to know whether their business idea will work and we always start any one-on-one business coaching by crunching numbers to assess risk vs. potential success. To set people up for organizational as well as financial success, I also recommend spending some time considering the systems involved in the day-to-day running of a business.

Crunching the numbers

The concept of budgeting is not a thrilling one, but it doesn't need to be overwhelming. To be sure you'll have money for the electricity bills, begin with this simple assessment: figure out how much you need to live on each year. Be detailed and realistic and don't forget the annual or occasional expenses like taxes, insurance, car repairs, etc. Then assess your competition—what are others in the area charging, and what services do they provide? An internet search backed by phone calls to others in your area (you can ask a friend to call for you if you feel uncomfortable) will give you plenty to go on. Use this information to determine your own rates. Now estimate a reasonable, conservative number of clients per month and year, being careful to consider seasonal variables. Then do the math—does it add up?

If the numbers don't look initially promising, don't give up—go back to the drawing board to see what kind of creative solutions you can come up with. You might add another service to increase revenue, such as adding walking services to a training or sitting business. Bringing in an independent contractor or employee (see Chapter 7 for guidelines) can increase volume and thus income. Or think about a new approach to services already available in your area. For example, if other trainers are seeing clients once a week in their homes and teaching them to work their own dogs, you may be able to charge more for the convenience and efficiency of owner absent day training (but be sure to teach the owners what they need to know to keep the training intact).

Start-up capital is another consideration. For most dog pro businesses little is needed. Trainers usually work from a home office. In this case, the main expenses will be start-up support and marketing which, as you'll see in Chapter 4, do not need to be excessive. For a training business you might plan for somewhere in the neighborhood of $1,500 to $6,000 for an average low budget start up, not including education costs. Walkers and sitters, you have the same expenses plus investment in an appropriate vehicle if you don't already own one. Daycare operators and trainers wishing to open training facilities will experience much higher start-up costs, as they must factor in a building lease or purchase, any build-out construction costs, technology infrastructure, and materials. These expenses depend on too many variables—local real estate rates, the condition of your chosen space, your build-out vision, the complexity of your services, etc.—to provide an average cost range. But you can work with a real estate agent, contractor, and business advisor to generate accurate numbers for your own situation.

See the Resources for a detailed chart comparing start-up and ongoing costs, as well as many additional factors. You will also find a basic budget outline and business plan information.

Create effective systems from the beginning

Though it may be tempting to start taking clients and see what happens, you're best served by setting up systems from the beginning for things like client intake, billing, client homework instructions, policies and procedures, etc. You will probably adjust them as you grow, but having systems to begin with will make things smoother as you get your first client calls and as business picks up. It will also increase your look of professionalism. See Chapter 6 for more details on policies and the Resources for help with paperwork.

To the extent possible, avoid making decisions that are "just for now." If you have a desire or intention to expand your business later—to open a facility or add a service you aren't yet ready to provide, for example—

keep that in mind as you start your business. Don't make decisions that will have to be undone later. Take your present and future into account when doing things such as choosing a business name, working on your marketing, creating your systems, defining your geographic service area, and setting up your business legally. For example, you wouldn't want to call yourself "Cuddles Pet Sitting" if your goal is to eventually become a trainer and help people with aggression issues. And a system of keeping client contact information in each person's folder will mean a lot of data entry later when you realize you need your contact information in a centralized location for ease of marketing. Or, before you take a dog walking or pet sitting client two towns away because you feel you should "take everything you can get at the beginning," stop to consider the stress of having to let those clients go later on, or the consequences of accidentally building a strong word of mouth business in the wrong place.

CASE STUDY

Adam was delighted with his dog walking business. He enjoyed a client waiting list and had far exceeded his financial expectations. But he was exhausted. He and his employees were running up huge gas bills and everyone felt like the proverbial chicken without a head. The systems Adam used to screen and schedule clients, and his policy of allowing part time clients, meant that every walker in his business walked slightly different packs each day and put in extra miles picking up dogs that lived across town from each other. This had all worked fine in the beginning, but now that his business was running at full capacity, the inefficiency was causing too much extra work. Adam put several changes into play. He reworked the packs to group dogs by geography (being careful to make sure they were temperamentally suited to each other, too!) and sent a letter to clients letting them know that beginning in the new year billing would be done at the beginning of each month to "reserve" their dog's full time spot in the pack, even if they didn't go out every day. For clients who had been used to part time, he offered to help find alternatives if they chose not to move to full time status. Adam was relieved to find that only a few decided to move on. Most understood the value of his service and were happy to commit, and the open spots were quickly filled from the waiting list. By the end of January, Adam happily reported that he was working far fewer hours for the same income.

Get professional help with your business

Some dog pros are experienced business people who have chosen to open a dog business, but most have never run a business before themselves and, as noted previously, it is often the only option available to make a living working with dogs. One secret to success in business is to do what you do well and get help with the rest. So if you're not a business person by trade or instinct, get some support to help ensure your success. Almost everyone will need the services of a good bookkeeper or accountant, an attorney, and an insurance agent as will be discussed in Chapter 3. Learn from colleagues, join professional organizations, and consider hiring a coach. There are resources you can tap listed at the back of this book.

Chapter 3

LEGALITIES AND LIABILITY

Is there a pit in your stomach as you open up this chapter? Be assured it'll be gone by the time you finish reading. Legalizing and protecting your business is so much easier—and comes at a far more reasonable price— than you might have feared. A little time spent now will allow you to work with the dogs in the comfort and security that comes from knowing your paperwork is in order and your assets are protected from lawsuits.

Legal requirements

Business license
Your business license is a permit from your city to do business within their borders, and is typically easy and inexpensive to acquire. Expect to pay on average $40-$150 per year. Application forms are usually between one and three pages long with straightforward questions. If your city asks for your yearly revenue or similar numbers you're unsure of, just give your best guess.

To pursue your license, begin at your city's website. Search for '[Your City] home page' on any search engine—and it will come up. Most city sites have downloadable business license application forms—some even let you apply online. Sometimes the downloadable forms come with instructions; sometimes they are separate or exist only on the website. Wherever they are, read them thoroughly before filling out the application.

If you intend to run your business from home you may need a zoning exemption. Cities designate neighborhoods for particular uses. In an area zoned for residential use you will need to file zoning exemption paperwork with your business license. This is usually a simple form in which you show that you won't significantly impact your neighborhood by putting up signage or having clients coming and going at all hours, for example. If administrative work is all you'll be doing—the basic phone and computer tasks—you should receive the exemption easily. Often, it's anything but obvious from a city's website that a zoning exemption is required, so check carefully. Even if you find nothing on the site, it's worth calling their help number to make sure—filing the exemption paperwork is much less complicated if your business license application hasn't been turned down once for zoning reasons.

Do you have to have a business license? Technically, yes. What happens if you don't? In most cases, nothing. In the worst case, large fines. Cities generally don't go searching for businesses operating without licenses, and if they find out at all it will likely only be due to a complaint about your business. But given that having a license is required by law and that it's simple to get (plan to spend an hour or two on the whole process) and usually costs little, it's certainly worth your while. What's more, it professionalizes and legitimizes your business and gives you one less thing to worry about.

Fictitious or assumed business name

The fictitious business name (FBN) sometimes goes by other monikers, such as an assumed business name (ABN) or a doing business as certificate (DBA). These are all the same thing. You don't need a fictitious business name if you are using your own name, e.g. Lisa Smith's Dog Training, to run your business. But if you plan to operate under a name other than your own, such as "Good Dog Training," you need to file this paperwork with your county clerk's office. As with the business license, the FBN application process is simple and inexpensive—usually around $40-$80 in total.

Registering a fictitious business name does two things. It announces to your community who is responsible for your business. This practice prevents people from setting up businesses and using them for nefarious activities while hiding their actual identities. To accomplish the announcement part of your fictitious, business name you have to publish a short statement about the creation and ownership of your business for a certain number of weeks in a local paper. When you file for your FBN you'll receive information about this requirement. Generally, a local paper or two will contact you and offer to take care of this step for you. In most cases the $40-$80 for your FBN includes this cost, though you will pay the newspaper separately.

The second purpose of the FBN is to avoid a confusing duplication of business names in the community—two businesses in one county called Good Dog Training is impractical.

To apply for your FBN search the internet for "[Your County] clerk's office." Once on the site, look for any reference to "business" or "fictitious business name" or "filings." Many county clerk sites allow you to search online to check that the business name you wish to register is available. If they don't, you may be able to call and ask them to do a search for you over the phone. In some cases you still need to go to your county clerk's office to do the search in person at a computer station or—gulp!—on microfiche. But this is rare. Once you've determined the name is available, you fill out the application—online if you can, or by downloading the form and mailing it in. In some places you have to apply in person, but this is unusual. Read the directions carefully—FBNs are often required to be submitted in multiple copies. But the paperwork itself is generally simple—rarely longer than two pages.

A quick note—if you are struggling with choosing a business name, see Chapter 4 for some help.

Service mark
While your fictitious business name protects your name in your own county, other dog professionals can use the same name elsewhere. If you wish to protect your name and/or logo further you can opt for a service mark, which is a trademark for a service oriented business. A service mark gives you exclusive rights to use a certain name and/or logo image to sell your services. A trademark would do the same thing for selling a physical product.

Service marks come in two sizes: the state level and the federal. Most state service mark applications require minimal paperwork (around two simple pages, plus you have to submit a sample of your name and/or logo in use—such as on a business card). State service marks tend to be inexpensive, too. So if you are very fond of your chosen name and/or image and plan to spend time, energy, and considerable capital promoting your business, you might give some consideration to a state service mark. An application form and directions can be downloaded from your secretary of state website by searching for "[Your State] Secretary of State home page."

A federal service mark is a bit more complicated and costly. The current fee is $375 and the paperwork is often difficult to navigate on one's own, though it certainly can be done. Technically you should be working across state lines in order to qualify for a federal mark. And while the federal mark holds more power than the state mark, it is unlikely a national company will come knocking on your door if you only operate regionally. Just don't name your business Petsmart!

In short, unless you are considering a national agenda that involves franchising, writing a book or widely syndicated column, going on the speaker circuit, etc., you don't need a national mark. But if you have plans for a future empire, a national service mark is essential. To check name availability, go to www.uspto.gov (the United States Patent and Trademark Office) to do an online search. You can also download an application form, but in that case it's a good idea to purchase a guidebook for support in filling out the paperwork. See the Resources at the back of the book.

URLs
Web addresses, or domain names, have to be purchased. Even if you apply for all the service marks and your FBN, someone else can still own the domain name you want. For this reason, it's advisable to search the internet for your chosen name before you proceed further. Do the search even if you don't mean to set up a website at this time. You will almost certainly want a site later and without a doubt potential clients will look for you online. Don't let them find someone else! Purchasing a domain name is inexpensive and easy. One last tip: Once you've found a name you like and made sure it's available, purchase all the domains you can. Most people use the .com address, but purchasing .info, .biz, .net, etc. as well is a low-cost way to reduce the chances that someone else will use your business name.

A Word on the Internet
If having a presence on the internet is new to you, here is a quick primer: Your website is like a large, online brochure. It is your marketing vehicle. Your web address, or domain name, is where you park your vehicle—it's where your website lives on the internet: www.yourbusinessnamehere.com. Your email address is how people reach you on the internet. In this case, You@yourbusinessnamehere.com.

FEIN
The FEIN, or Federal Employer Identification Number (sometimes shortened to just EIN), is like a social security number for your business.

If you are going to have employees, you'll need one. You'll also need one if you decide to become a limited liability company (see below), even if you never plan to hire employees.

Remarkably, even though this little number comes from the IRS, it is free and easy to get. Simply go to www.irs.gov and do a search for form SS-4. It's a single straightforward page with a number to call to get help. Or you can call and get your EIN over the phone in about 5 minutes. If only the IRS were always so helpful! Find additional contact information in the Resources at the back of this book.

Liability issues

For anyone who is or is planning to be a dog professional, knowing the risks involved in your profession is essential, as are the steps you can take to professionalize and protect yourself.

How big is the risk?

Dog professions are often thought of as high risk because—simply put—dogs are animals and animals bite. But how great is the risk actually? Unfortunately there are no official legal statistics kept to help us answer this question. Anecdotally, in my seven years of experience working with dog pros across the country, first as Director of Behavior & Training for the San Francisco SPCA and then through dogTEC, I am aware of only three high profile lawsuits and I personally know no one who has been sued as a dog professional. And the fact that insurance policy rates for dog professionals are surprisingly low suggests that insurance companies do not experience a high rate of liability protection claims. But there certainly is more risk in working with dogs than making and selling pottery, and it makes sense to protect yourself and your business.

For one thing, if you do happen to find yourself on the unpleasant end of a lawsuit, the financial, professional, and emotional results could be very damaging. Lawsuits are stressful and can be costly. For another, we live in a litigious society. As our profession grows and the media continues to highlight and sensationalize dog bites, public awareness increases as well and some people are always going to be influenced by sensationalism. In fact, more worrisome to me than the actual statistics of lawsuits are the anecdotal signs that lawyers are seeing dog bites as potentially lucrative. Recently, the front cover of a large California Bay Area phone book proclaimed the services of a father-and-daughter law team specializing in dog bite cases. Clearly they smell an income growth area and their enthusiasm may prove contagious.

Still, there's no need to worry. A few simple steps now and you'll have the peace of mind to fully enjoy your work with dogs. And yes, if you've been in business for a while—even years—you can simply make the changes now and be more secure. Protecting yourself is easy and there is simply no good reason not to.

Think of the three things you can do to protect your liability as three layers of safety nets you rig between yourself and any legal trouble. You'll want your nets arranged in descending order of strength: contracts, insurance, and limited liability company status.

Contracts

A good contract with every client is your first safety net. A strong contract includes two things: (1) a section specifying any key information about the dog and the care you are to provide; and (2) effective waiver language that clearly spells out what you are and are not responsible for.

The key information might include things like medical issues, behavioral issues, and the specific services you will perform. Have yourself and the client sign off on anything that could be a potential issue in the future. For example, food allergies, behavioral problems, or service details. It would be a shame to find out too late that a dog in your care was allergic to chicken or was fearful of and likely to snap at children, or that a client was expecting you to take their dog for two walks a day when you thought you were to provide one. Worse yet would be a client that claimed he told you about the allergy or behavior problem or their two-walk expectation when you know different. A good contract, then, is a legal record of what you did and did not know.

The waiver language portion of the contract is language that spells out the areas of responsibility held by you and by your client. Typically this section has specific legal language that protects you in the event of accidental damage to the dog or any persons.

To obtain a good contract with legal waiver language, you can contact friendly colleagues to see if they might be willing to share theirs, draft one yourself, or purchase a contract from a professional organization that supports dog pros (see Resources).

However you obtain one, it is always a good idea to have your attorney go through the contract to make sure it is as tight and effective as possible for your specific use. This approach is far less expensive than having a lawyer draft the paperwork from scratch.

A few tips:

- Use a contract with every client.

- Use a fresh contract when old clients come back for additional services.

- Make sure both you and the client sign and date the contract.

- Keep your contracts filed in a safe place.

Although contracts are important they are only your first line of defense. For better or worse, our country affords all citizens the right to sue and no matter how strong a contract is, understand a person cannot sign away this right. Nonetheless contracts act as an excellent deterrents. Many people don't realize having signed a contract does not limit their legal recourse and those who do typically understand that having signed the contract renders their arguments much weaker. It's hard for a client to claim that she told a trainer her dog was reactive to children when the "Behavior Issues" section of the contract she signed is blank! Should a problem arise, the presence of a signed contract lowers the chances of actually going to court or having to pay for any real or perceived damages.

Insurance

Sometimes we make mistakes despite our best intentions. So in addition to contracts, all dog pros should have a strong insurance policy. Insurance is your second safety net should the first one fail. Luckily, and perhaps surprisingly, dog pro insurance is easy to obtain and remarkably low-cost.

To access a group liability insurance policy you need only belong to a professional organization such as the Association of Pet Dog Trainers (APDT) or Pet Sitters International (PSI). Membership to these organizations is as simple as going to their websites and signing up. Their fees typically fall in the neighborhood of $100 per year, and usually come with nice perks such as newsletters and referral lists.

A million dollars in liability coverage costs roughly $350 per year for dog walkers and pet sitters and $350-$500 per year for trainers depending on the services you provide (training in a client's home vs. boarding, for example) and whether you have a training facility. Daycares, expect to pay $500-$1,000 per year. This cost is stunningly low considering the perception of our industry as high risk, especially given the protection and peace of mind it affords.

To clarify, liability insurance covers your risks for your work as a dog pro. It is separate from any personal medical insurance you carry and from any homeowner's or renter's policies. I am often asked if liability insurance can be obtained through a homeowner's or renter's policy. Unfortunately the answer is no.

A final, important word on liability insurance—not all policies are created equal. The most crucial difference among policies is that many do not cover "after contract." Imagine that a couple hires you to help with their dog, Benji. Benji is lovely but is dog reactive when walked on leash. You spend six sessions working with Benji and her people. Two months after your last session Benji has a dog-dog incident while out on a walk and the result is a redirected bite to the other dog's owner, who got his hand too close. The other dog's owner sues Benji's parents, who in turn sue you, claiming they were following your instructions when the bite happened. Perhaps your lawyer advises you to settle and you turn to your insurance company for support, only to find that the fine print clearly (or not so clearly, as the case may be!) states that your policy covers only while you are under active contract with a client. The lesson is to be careful when choosing your insurance carrier—ask whether a policy covers after contract. And don't assume that because one of the prominent professional organizations offers access to a particular company that their policy covers after contract—they often don't. The good news, though, is that your professional association membership gives you access to multiple policies, not just the one the association may be partnered with. Additional insurance information can be found in the Resources.

Limited liability companies

Becoming a limited liability company (LLC) is your third available safety net. The most common way to be in business is to be a sole proprietor or partnership. A sole proprietorship is a business owned by one person and it is the default mode of doing business. If you don't actively decide to be something else, you're automatically a sole proprietor. A partnership is the same thing, except with more than one person.

The chief advantage of being a sole proprietor or partnership is simplicity. As with any business you'll need a license and a fictitious business name, and should carry insurance. You'll have to keep track of your financial records and pay taxes. But that's it—there's no other paperwork and it is the simplest form of business for taxes, too—what the business makes, you make. What the business loses, you report as a loss. Pretty simple.

But the simplicity of doing business as a sole proprietor or partnership has its downside, too. The law and the IRS see a sole proprietor and her business as the same legal entity. That's why taxes and paperwork are so minimal. But being the same legal entity also means that when the business is in trouble, you are, too. If there's a lawsuit it's not just your business assets at risk—it's anything you own personally. So your property, trust fund, bank account, etc. can be at risk. When selling widgets this risk is minimal, working with animals with teeth is a little dicier.

To avoid this risk many businesses organize themselves as corporations. Unlike sole proprietorships or partnerships, corporations are considered separate legal entities from their owners. If the business encounters trouble it stays with the business. A protective brick wall, if you will, has been raised between owners and their corporations. This wall affords liability protection and potential tax breaks. Unfortunately corporations come with a major disadvantage for most dog businesses: they are complicated to run, as they are required in most states to have a board of directors that meets and files minutes at least once per year, and to issue stock to stock holders. This is a lot more work and hassle than most dog trainers are interested in. And the catch is that if you don't follow through on these matters properly your protective brick wall crumbles. You can't just file a corporation application—you have to act like a corporation to be treated like one.

Fortunately, since the late 1980s the LLC has been sanctioned in all 50 states as a way to help small and medium-sized businesses enjoy the advantages of sole proprietorships and corporations without the disadvantages of either. An LLC delivers the simplicity and the liability protection in one package.

LLCs are simple to form and can be comprised of just one person or many. Each state has its own application form and fees. The application form is rarely longer than two pages. Fees vary widely from state to state—from $40-$500. Some states have yearly renewal fees, some do not. Most yearly renewal fees are low. (California residents have the added burden of an $800/year state tax.) By default, LLCs are taxed the same way as a sole proprietorship, but you can opt to be taxed as a corporation. Consult a tax accountant familiar with small businesses, LLCs, and corporations to find the right taxation scheme for you. This is best done before becoming an LLC, as part of determining whether it's the best option for you and to make sure you have the information you need to act properly as an LLC. LLCs have far fewer requirements than a corporation, but they must be followed for the safety net to work.

Given the fees involved in your state (or the tax in CA), should you become an LLC? Only you can answer that, but here are some things to consider:

- What is your risk level? Are you pet sitting cats in their homes or teaching puppy classes? Or are you walking dogs off leash or working with aggressive dogs?

- What do you stand to lose? Are you just out of college with little to your name, ready to launch your first career? Or are you married with a home and retirement investments, pursuing your dream job?

- What is your risk comfort level? Are you the trainer who believes the lawsuit will never find you, of all people? Or are you the dog walker who worries each night before falling into a fretful sleep that tomorrow will be the day?

Put your answers to each of these questions in one hand, and the fees involved in your state in the other, and judge which feels heaviest. If you decide to pursue LLC status, search for your state's secretary of state website—you'll almost certainly find a downloadable application there. You will also find additional resources in the back of this book.

CASE STUDY

Sharon and Rebecca traded notes after the LLC workshop. Sharon leaned toward transitioning her business to an LLC. "With the kids getting ready for college and the house almost paid off—it just seems like a good idea. I think I would feel safer with my aggression cases, for sure." Rebecca, just out of college, had a different perspective. "I don't know," she told Sharon. "I think I'll just be a sole proprietor, especially while I'm only doing puppy classes. I'm not making enough to worry about yet, and I can't imagine anyone would want my lame old car! I don't think my pockets are deep enough to worry about!"

What to do if you've been operating without all this stuff

What if you've been in business for awhile without all this in place? No reason to fret—you can remedy the situation now. But don't delay. Setting aside the time is a bother, the fees are irksome, and facing the paperwork can be stressful. But the greater professionalism and peace of mind are well worth it.

Here are some tips for catching up on the issues covered in this chapter:

Business license
This is probably the trickiest item to get after the fact. I'd advise you to call the city (anonymously) and find out what their policy is for retroactive business licenses. If it looks like you'll have a large fee to pay you can decide whether to apply with your original start date or from this date forward.

FBN
Find out first whether your county has fees for filing late. Most likely they do not, but knowing this ahead of time can inform what date you use on your paperwork.

Service marks
There is no issue with filing now, as this process is optional. The only consequence in delaying is that someone else might file for the same name before you do.

FEIN
The only potential problem here is if you have hired employees without properly reporting them, but that would fall outside the scope of this book. See the Resources for additional information on this issue.

Contracts
Just start using them as soon as possible. The only consequence of not having used them up until now is that you aren't as well covered should something come up with a past client.

Insurance
You can apply for insurance at any time. There will be no retroactive fees unless, that is, you can convince your agent to insure you retroactively.

LLC
There is no consequence to filing now other than not being as well protected in the past as you will be in the future. You can convert an existing sole proprietorship or partnership into an LLC any time you wish.

CASE STUDY
Tai spent the morning screwing up her courage for the phone call. "Well, I've been walking dogs for about four years. My business is doing well and I really enjoy it, but well..." Here she took a deep breath. "Okay, I've never had a business license or insurance or anything like that—I don't even know for sure what I'm supposed to have. I didn't mean to go so long without doing all

this stuff. I just didn't get to it and then time passed and then I was afraid to find out what I should have done and how much trouble I'd be in that I hadn't. But I worry all the time while I'm out there with the dogs and I just can't take it anymore!" I was happy to tell Tai that it was not too late to put legal requirements and liability protections in place. With some support she got everything in order in no time. Now Tai enjoys her daily hikes with the dogs without her daily worries.

Order of operations: When to do what

In the Resources there are annotated To-Do Lists, with all the steps from this and others chapters laid out in order.

The order of operations is important because some paperwork requires that other paperwork has been filed first. For example, your city business license form may ask for your FBN certification—or it may be the other way around in your county. So download all paperwork and instructions and read through for cross-references. The To-Do List at the back will give you the most standard and conservative order to follow.

Chapter 4

BUILD IT AND THEY WILL COME? YOU NEED A MARKETING PLAN!

Common wisdom holds that only 10-20% of businesses in the United States survive their first two years. But data for 2005 from the Bureau of Labor Statistics tell a better story—that 44% of businesses are still in operation after four years. That's good news, but you still have to make sure you're on the right side of that statistic. One crucial element that sets those 44% apart from the rest is good marketing, a concept that involves a lot more than printing up a stack of business cards to leave around town. You need to develop an effective marketing message, including a visual look for your business, and a plan for getting that message out there. But marketing doesn't have to be intimidating, complicated, or costly—it just needs to be creative and thoughtful. And most importantly, it needs to be done.

Find your message

To build a marketing plan you need to know what you have to offer. How will you convince dog owners that you are the dog pro they need? Existing isn't good enough—you have to give them a reason to call you.

Marketing maxim #1: Find your niche

What makes you special? One of the most common marketing mistakes dog pros make is to generalize. If you're the only game in town, it makes sense to tell potential clients that you do it all. But if there are multiple dog pros in your area, what will make a client call you instead of someone else? Don't leave it to chance. Give them a reason to call you by marketing a specialization. Find a niche and fill it well.

First, take a look at what the competition in your area is doing. Think about what you might have to offer that is different. For example, do you have any skills from a former career or hobby that might serve as a nice complement to your services? For example, if you are an avid runner you might offer dog runs for young, rowdy, athletic dogs instead of walks. Or a previous career working with children might be applied to a dog training business focused on working with families. Consider your preferences, too. Do you enjoy working with puppies or small dogs? Is there a training issue you are particularly good at handling? Who are your ideal clients? You might also consider any services not currently being offered that could be of use to dog owners in your area, such as pick up and drop off services, group dog walks, or small dog playgroups.

Having a niche gives a subsection of potential clients a reason to call you over every other service provider in your area. These clients then tell their friends and family and co-workers about you, and you begin to build your business. Of course you can absolutely be a generalist, too. Say you're a trainer specializing in treating separation anxiety, and your marketing efforts predictably bring you clients with separation anxiety problems. If you help solve those problems, it is likely the client will refer you to friends and family for any training needs they have. Even with a particularly narrow niche focus you can expect a good half of your clients to fall outside your specialty.

CASE STUDIES

Cindy had burned out working as a vet tech in a high-pressure vet hospital, and decided to start her own pet sitting business. The number of people already pet sitting in her area intimidated her, but her vet tech expertise made her worries unnecessary. She directed her business at owners with older and ill pets, explaining that she would be able to care both for their emotional and physical well being, including administering medicines, IVs, and any other home medical care required. She networked with veterinary offices and other pet sitters and was soon overwhelmed with referrals for clients needing special care for their elderly, infirm, or injured animals while away.

Ruth Anne found her skills as a dog trainer very useful while preparing her young dog for the arrival of her first baby and after she brought the baby home. She noticed several of the women in her new moms' group were struggling with their dogs and babies, and a niche was born. Ruth Anne changed the name of her business to Beagles and Babies and began marketing to expectant and new moms through groups, pediatricians, and the Infant and Parent Group program at her two local hospitals. She also developed curricula for two public dog training classes, one for expectant parents and one for new parents. Her business is thriving.

Before moving to the city, Margot owned a successful home-based dog training and boarding business. After getting married and moving to a small place in a big city, Margot wondered how she would make board and train work. Then she noticed all the small dogs coming and going from the high-end apartment and condominium complexes around the city. Margot built a business around training and boarding services for small dogs only. Her marketing plan included networking with local small dog rescue groups, groomers, and high-end doggie boutique stores. Her message of special care for the smalls, which included a home-like environment and healthy training treats, hit home with small dog owners and she now maintains a wait list for her services.

A Word On Business Names

It's hard to find a name that says it all, especially if you offer multiple services. It's worth spending some time searching for the perfect fit, but don't obsess, and don't allow it to distract or delay you. The marketing you do and the quality of your service will far outweigh the importance of your name. Far more important than creating an ingenious name is to find a niche and market to it.

Some dog pros opt to use their own names rather than a business name. That's fine, too. Both approaches have advantages. A personal name suggests direct service. A business name carries the connotation of an established, professional company.

Marketing maxim #2: Market to your clients, not yourself

Remember that your marketing message is for your potential clients—be sure to please them, rather than yourself. Because we dog pros are so passionate about what we do, it's a universal mistake to forget clients when building a marketing message. For example, you might feel strongly about teaching people to train their own dogs. But before using the slogan "We Train You to Train Fido," stop to think whether that is what your potential clientele is looking for. Most people hire a trainer because they have a problem they want solved—a behavior they want stopped or one they wish they had more of. If you find a way to let potential clients know you can help to solve their problem, they're more likely to hire you.

And if they hire you, you'll still have your chance to teach them how to train their own dog.

> ## CASE STUDY
>
> Maria's website announced that she helped dog owners "build a terrific relationship" with their dogs. It was a beautiful website and her proclaimed goal was no doubt a worthy one. Still, though she watched the visit count to her site rise, she found that few of her visitors called or emailed. Given Maria's specialization in aggression cases, she had a strong niche to put to work. So she re-focused her website and other materials around the message of efficient and effective problem solving to meet client goals. Now both Maria and her phone find themselves quite a bit busier, and Maria is achieving her goal of helping people with their aggressive dogs—and their relationships with them.

You might make an exception to this rule if you have a strong desire to pre-screen clients for certain messages or services. For example, if you only want to work with people looking for a trainer to help them train their own dogs, rather than clients looking to have their dogs trained for them, then "We Train You to Train Fido" is a great marketing message.

> ## CASE STUDY
>
> During the first couple years of owning her training business, Denise was surprised to find the work so emotionally taxing. She was uncomfortable discussing training methodologies with potential clients, and got upset with clients who were not sold on positive reinforcement (R+) approaches. By the end of her second year she considered leaving the profession, even though she loved training. Instead she changed all her marketing materials to very clearly state her R+ approach. Now, most dog owners who call her are searching specifically for a positive trainer, and Denise appreciates her work again.

Marketing maxim #3: Emphasize benefits

Don't just tell people what you do. Tell them why they should work with you. A list of services isn't nearly as compelling as a list of benefits. Instead of telling them in a bullet point that you treat separation anxiety, ask them to imagine being able to safely leave their dog at home while they enjoy an evening out. Instead of telling them that you walk dogs, point out that using a dog walker means having a calm dog to come home to after work. It's easy to forget to do this. When I first started dogTEC our tagline was "Continuing Education. Professional Support." Contrast that with "Our business is to help yours succeed." Our first try just listed what we do in the vaguest of terms, whereas the revision communicates the benefit—a successful business.

Marketing maxim #4: Know your audience

Knowing your market is an important part of choosing an effective marketing message and visual identity. Who are the clients you're hoping will call you? Are they men, women, families, seniors, young professionals, college educated, middle class? What do they need—problem behaviors fixed or a polite social dog, a quick potty break or a well exercised dog, someone to check in on their pup, or someone to stay overnight? Where do you find them? Where do they get their dog information? Where do they hang out? What do they read? Finding out as much of this information as possible will help you to make informed marketing decisions. You may enjoy designs that are on the pink girly side, but if your potential clients are primarily middle-aged professionals you might want to go for something more upscale and gender neutral. And if you know that the majority of your potential clients will be families with children you might consider incorporating that information into your marketing plan by focusing on helping families discover the Lassie in their Lab, Lhasa, or mutt.

CASE STUDY

David did his homework. Upon learning that his neighborhood church was 2,500 families strong with a high median income and lots of dog ownership, David contacted the minister about a humane education program for children and families. Teaching his program on Sunday afternoons created terrific exposure and helped to establish David as the local dog expert, eventually leading to a steady stream of clients.

For most dog pro businesses, a formal market study isn't necessary. Just take a look around and do some thinking. For example, it's easy to find out the median income in your area with a quick internet search or call to the local chamber of commerce. But you can also look at the houses people live in and the cars they drive to draw conclusions about socio-economic status. If you require accurate statistics for a formal business plan for funding, there are website services that can help. See the Resources at the back of the book.

Another approach is to decide who you want your clients to be, and then gear your materials toward that profile. You may, for example, decide you want to concentrate on the most affluent members of your community. Or if you prefer to work with families, let that guide you.

Having said all this, make certain you please yourself, too. Don't opt for a message or look that doesn't appeal to you—it's hard to sell something you don't buy!

CASE STUDY

Wendy found her dog walking niche not in a particular type of service or dog, but in her potential client base. Looking around her community she found that among all the various groups, those identifying themselves gay had the highest income, highest dog ownership, and the highest spending per dog. "They seemed like the perfect clients to me—dedicated to their dogs and able to afford services for them." So she targeted her marketing through the local gay newspaper and dog oriented businesses in targeted neighborhoods, to good effect. She has a terrific referral rate and is enjoying her work. "I love my clients," Wendy says. "They are enthusiastic, educated, and devoted to their dogs!"

Get the word out

Marketing maxim #5: Market!

You now have a message. But what do you do with it? How do you get the word out there? Although you can grow a business by unprompted word of mouth alone, it takes a long time. Somebody has to do the talking—how do you get that first wave of clients?

This is where most businesses fly or fail. The fifth maxim of marketing, the most important one, is simple enough: You have to market yourself. Too many dog pros make up a few business cards, leave them around town, and then wait for the phone to ring. But there is an ocean of business cards strewn around coffee shops and pet supply stores—how many of them do you pay attention to?

What to do, then? Begin by considering your strengths—what do you do well and enjoy? Are you a good public speaker? Are you better working with small group or as a one-on-one teacher? How's your writing? What about your planning skills?

Now consider your environment. What other dog-related businesses are around? Vets, groomers, supply stores and boutiques, shelters and rescue groups? Oh—and don't forget other trainers, walkers, and sitters, too! They can be a terrific networking resource. What about local activities? Are there dog parks or local festivals, adult education or community classes? And what are local folks reading—any local dailies or weeklies or monthlies? In short, what's going on in your neighborhood?

CASE STUDY

Robert had just graduated from dog training school and was contemplating the intimidating task of starting a new training business in a market saturated with dog trainers and walkers. On top of that, he wasn't yet feeling confident enough in his training skills to just jump in. But a good niche coupled with professional networking solved both problems. Robert set up a business walking difficult dogs, dogs not behaviorally suitable for other walkers and daycares. And, rather than marketing directly to the public, he marketed to the other trainers, walkers, and daycare businesses in the area. Soon he had a full schedule of dogs referred by daycares and other walkers and trainers.

Marketing maxim #6: Use creativity, not cash
You've got your niche, a list of your strengths, and a list of local places and activities. Now it's time to get creative.

This brings us to our sixth marketing maxim: Creativity over cash. It's not that money can't be a great help to a marketing plan—of course it can—but most dog pros don't possess large amounts of start-up capital. And the reality is that a little cash doesn't go a long way in marketing. So if you don't have the big bucks your creativity can stand in nicely.

As you scan your two lists, you're looking for good potential match ups between your skill sets on the one side and the resources or potential opportunities on the other. If you enjoy writing, perhaps the local neighborhood weekly would like to run a regular "Ask the Trainer" column. A dog walker with good writing skills might offer an article about the benefits of dog walking, a pet sitter on how to pick a sitter. What terrific exposure, at no cost! And so much more effective than running an ad, especially when you're attempting to sell yourself. A column establishes your expertise and credibility. You become the sought-after local expert. Or, if you're a trainer specializing in helping people with puppies and new dogs, wouldn't it be great if the local shelter recommended you to all of their adopters?

CASE STUDIES

Tasha couldn't help notice as she walked her pack of client dogs every day how messy the dog park had gotten—trash, untended piles of feces—it was unsightly and, she felt, gave dogs, dog owners, and dog professionals a bad name. Seeing an opportunity to do something for her community and her dog walking business, she worked with the parks department to co-sponsor, organize, and promote a Dog Park Clean Up Day. The park got cleaned up, her business got lots of free press, including an article in the local paper and a short spot on the local evening news, and Tasha got several new clients.

Hilary had been trying for some time to network with her local shelter. The shelter had good standing in the community and was viewed as a source of training and veterinary knowledge, but they did not provide private training services. She knew they were short staffed and thought both she and they could benefit from a referral service. She decided to leave her cards on the front desk counter, but it seemed they were rarely given out, and she hardly ever received referrals. Then she offered to help answer the shelter behavior hotline. Together with the behavior manager, she set up a triage system for incoming calls to take pressure off the shelter staff. They determined which calls the staff could easily handle and forwarded the more difficult calls to Hilary. Hilary was careful to limit the time of each call, providing some immediately applicable management advice, and then scheduling a consult with anyone interested. The hotline is now Hilary's number one source of clients.

Marketing maxim #7: Create relationships

Writing a local column and getting shelter referrals are great marketing goals—but how do you make these things happen?

This brings us to another oft-made mistake in marketing training businesses: Asking instead of giving. As I said before, the typical marketing plan includes drawing up business cards to post around other dog-oriented businesses. Often we ask the business owners if we can put our cards on their bulletin boards or in a holder on their counters. If brave enough we might even introduce ourselves, talk a little about what we do, and ask for their referrals.

But ask yourself: Why should they? They don't know you or your abilities, they're busy, and you've given them no reason to want to help you, either. So rather than just asking for help, consider what you might have to offer.

If you'd like to write a regular column in the neighborhood paper, first try offering one article, already written, on a dog topic of broad interest. If you would like the shelter to refer their new adopters to you, put together a free adopter's package of articles or tip handouts that the shelter can give to its adopters. Make sure your name and business information is on all the handouts, and includes any of your other marketing material as well! And maybe they would appreciate some training for their staff—a small series of talks or hands-on seminars. These offerings allow the shelter to get to know you, to come to see you as an expert, and to build loyalty to you. Sure, you can leave your cards on the front counter and hope people pick them up and call, but you'll no doubt receive many more phone calls if the shelter staff is actively and enthusiastically sending adopters your way. And if you offer a free one-time class aimed at new doggie parents, so much the better—this is a direct opportunity for face time with potential clients!

CASE STUDY

Suzanne believed that an ounce of prevention was worth a pound of cure, especially when it comes to puppies and newly adopted dogs. She wanted to focus her business on getting people and dogs off on the right paw, but how to get the word out? The local shelter did a brisk adoption business, and Suzanne decided to start there. She offered to teach a free adopter's class at the shelter, at no cost to them. She gave the two-hour talk one evening each week, and the shelter scheduled that week's adopters into the lecture. Suzanne's talk covered the basics of setting up a home for a new dog, house training, and prevention of common behavior problems, and she always made sure to talk about her private training services as well. Her business grew steadily as she signed up occasional clients at the talks, and found that over time people who had attended her class called as they developed training problems, and often referred her to friends and family as well.

Marketing maxim #8: Be active, not passive
One reason giving a community talk or answering a shelter hotline are much more powerful marketing tools than simply placing materials around town or an ad in the paper are that they are examples of active marketing—opportunities for clients to interact with your business rather than just seeing it advertised. Instead of picking up a business card, a

shelter staff person hands your materials to potential clients while telling them, "You have to call this trainer. She is amazing and can help you fix this problem." If I post a flier on a bulletin board, there is no potential for active interaction between my business and my hoped-for clients. If instead I disseminate a quarterly newsletter to the same businesses, the people who pick it up have a more interactive experience with my business. Rather than a flier that lists "problem behavior solving" as one of my services, an article in each newsletter can highlight an issue and tell the story of one or more dogs and clients whose lives were changed by training. In that narrative they get to "see" an example of the benefits of your training and imagine themselves getting similar help, rather than just reading a bullet point.

A Word About Print Advertising

Not only is print advertising passive marketing, it is also expensive and generally has a low return on investment—meaning that it doesn't work that well. Although there are some exceptions, I generally advise people to try other avenues first. Why not do something that is free, active, and more likely to work— and work continuously over time? You might be an exception if you have a small local neighborhood paper because there is less chance for your ad to be lost in all the information and because people sometimes feel more loyalty toward small local businesses. Even so, an article would give you much more mileage—and it's free. Another exception would be if other dog pros in your area all advertise in one paper—in that case you might want a presence there, too. But an article would still trump all those other ads.

If you do decide to try print advertising, follow these three guidelines for success: Make sure your ad emphasizes benefits over product (remember Maxim #3!). Run your ad at least three times—repeat contact is key in print advertising. And be sure to keep track of any hits you get from the ad so you can gauge its success and decide whether to continue running it.

The success of phone book ads seems to vary, largely depending on whether you work in a competitive area. While it may seem anti-intuitive, the yellow pages appear to work best for dog pros in smaller communities with less competition. In a more saturated market a phone book ad can lead to plenty of phone ringing, but my clients and colleagues report that most of these inquiries don't turn into business. One theory is that the calls are fishing expeditions— people comparing prices, etc. If you live in an urban spot full of dog professionals it's more likely that serious potential clients will find you through active referrals from friends, family, and other dog businesses such as vets, retail stores, other dog pros, or shelters, or by coming across your article, newsletter, or community lecture. There are exceptions to this, of course, but as phone book ads carry a heavy price tag try more active, less expensive marketing avenues first.

Marketing maxim #9: Tell them again and again

A brochure is always the same. If I've picked it up once, I'm unlikely to pick it up again. Even if I do, there is no new input. A newsletter, on the other hand, encourages me to pick it up multiple times a year. Each time I read an article about a featured client and their dog I get another picture of what training, daycare, walking, or sitting could do for me, and a deepening sense of the writer as an expert. And a regular "Tips" article that I find interesting or helpful gives me a reason to hang onto my copies, maybe even put one on the fridge. Six months from now, when I find myself struggling with a new dog problem, I know who to call. And I'm more likely to find a copy of the newsletter around my house than a business card (if I even remember that I had the card). Or when my neighbor or friend or colleague mentions how much trouble their new puppy is, or how their dog is so bored during the day, I might tell them about the great dog pro who writes this newsletter.

Implement your marketing plan

Once you have your marketing plan, it's time to put it to work!

Marketing maxim #10: Develop materials for your plan, not the other way around

One of the first things many dog pros do upon deciding to start a business is to have business cards and brochures made, before doing any real thinking about the marketing plan itself. A common result? Boxes of brochures stored under the bed. It doesn't make sense to order brochures unless your marketing plan includes a clear role for them to play.

Once you've developed a message and designed some strategies to get that message out, you're ready to decide what materials you need and what they should look like and say.

CASE STUDY

Barbara was excited about starting her business. She wanted to get things going right away. The first thing she did was to hire a designer to help her with a logo, business cards, and a beautiful brochure. Two years later most of her brochures are gathering dust in her office closet. They look great, but she just hasn't had many opportunities to use them. As it turns out, most of her clients come from the training classes she set up through the local Parks and Recreation Department and the local community college, and then eventually from the referrals from those clients. Parks and Rec and the college do most the promotion for the classes and they're nearly always full, so she hasn't had much need for the brochures.

Let your marketing strategies determine what materials you will need. If you've decided to write a newsletter, you need a newsletter template. If you've decided to provide adopter's packets to the local shelter, you might have stickers made to go on the front of folders that hold your articles and tip sheets. In that case, professional letterhead to print those on would be helpful. Only get what you really need. Don't waste your resources purchasing materials that don't have a clear role in your marketing plan. Don't assume you need brochures just because everyone else has them.

Once you're clear about what you need, it's time to find a good designer, one who can create an entire branded image for you. Ask to see sample work from anyone you're considering. You can look in your phone book, do an internet search, or take a look at the Resources in the back of this book—I've listed some companies and designers that work specifically with dog businesses. You may be lucky enough to have a friend or family member who does graphic design work. But that luck comes with a downside, too, and be forewarned: I've worked with many clients suffering the frustration of waiting (and waiting and waiting) for that friend or brother or husband to finish their design work. Very often, no matter how sincere your friend or relative is, other more pressing matters may end up on top of their to-do list and you end up waiting longer than if you just hired the work out to a professional.

Once you find a designer, share your marketing message and strategies with her, and explain the materials you need. Typically a designer will show you a few ideas or paths to choose from and from there you select one to fine-tune. Or you can ask them to execute an idea of your own.

Regardless of what other materials you have, it also makes sense to have a web presence. For most dog pros, a small, simple website will do. One to five pages is plenty, and extra features like flash graphics are not necessary. As long as it looks polished and professional and you've presented your marketing message clearly, it will get the job done for you. Don't feel the need to have a large site unless it makes sense for your business and marketing plan. If you are opening a facility that offers multiple services, a more extensive site, perhaps featuring a class and events calendar and registration capability, might actually save you time.

Lastly, you may also consider hiring a writer to write or edit your marketing material for you. Even if you write well, a good writer with some marketing savvy can help your marketing message hit home. To find a writer do an internet search, look around locally, or take a look at the Resources at the back of this book.

Marketing maxim #11: Giving instead of asking: Make your offers

Once you have your materials it's time to start making the connections that will turn into your referral relationships. Remember when you contact people and businesses that you are a colleague with something of benefit to offer them. You're working toward a mutually beneficial goal. You are not a start-up asking plaintively for help. What you have to offer is of value.

How do you make the first contact? It all depends on the situation, but these days the answer is often email. Email has several advantages. It allows you time to deliberate on your language and get things just right. It eliminates the discomfort of a cold call or drop-in visit. It reaches the intended person at a time when he or she has time to consider it—presumably if they are reading email it's because they have a few quiet moments to do so. A first contact by email might be particularly good for contacting newspapers, veterinary offices, and other dog pros. In addition to introducing what you have to offer, ask for a good time to call or possibly to set up a time to talk by phone or in person.

Whatever format it takes, be sure to follow up that first contact if you don't hear back. Don't assume they aren't interested—life is busy and sometimes people aren't able to respond. So email again or call or, if appropriate, drop by to follow up.

Marketing maxim #12: Keep your message on target

As you carry out your marketing plan, stay on target with your message. Just as in working with dogs, consistency is key to success. Everything you do or say, and all of your visual and written materials, should reinforce your marketing message. A strong message will pull people in. Materials in which the message is weak or non-existent are a wasted opportunity.

CASE STUDY

A tragic childhood accident had brought a therapy dog into Lora's life, strongly influencing the course of her life and future career as a dog trainer. She featured the story prominently on her website and in her marketing materials, feeling that it could help clients form a personal connection with her. She eventually realized, though, that her story overshadowed her marketing message and the services she had to offer. She moved her story off her home page, and emphasized her ability to help people solve tough behavioral problems. On the Services page she focused on, yes, her services, and on the About the Trainer page her professional qualifications got the spotlight, with a shortened version of her story afterward. Although she had a compelling story to tell, Lora came to understand that potential clients seek a trainer to help them solve their own problems and that the best way to get those clients was to show them she was available to listen to their stories.

One tip for keeping your message strong is to be as succinct and to-the-point as possible. There are probably many things you could say about your business, but too many competing concepts drown out the central message.

Your marketing is only as strong as your weakest message point. Consider all the opportunities potential clients have to come into contact with your business—physical materials such as cards, brochures, fliers, and the like, word-of-mouth referrals, seeing your car go by with advertising panels, your outgoing phone message, your website, hearing you lecture, reading something you've written, and so on—these are message points. You want all of these to be polished, professional, and on target—even one off message point can discourage a potential client.

CASE STUDY

Debbie had all her marketing message ducks in a row—almost. Her website was beautifully designed. Her truck was always clean, allowing the signs on the side to announce her business. Her business cards were professionally done, her newsletter well written. And all were on target, broadcasting professionalism. Why, then, were there so few messages in her voice mail box? Finally, Debbie understood. She tossed out her old outgoing greeting: "Hi, this is Debbie, Stan, Maggie the Dog and Bill the Cat! We're sorry we can't come to the phone right now. For Debbie or Stan, press 1. For Maggie or Bill, press 2. If you need pet sitting, press 3. Have a super day!" She opted instead for a more professional tone: "You've reached Good Dog Pet Sitting. We're out caring for animals now, but look forward to returning your call. Please leave your name, number, and let us know how we can help care for your good dog." Debbie finds there are far fewer clicks on her answering machine these days.

Marketing maxim #13: Reinforce referrals

A little positive reinforcement goes a long way. Don't forget to reinforce referrals, whether from clients, other businesses you've networked with, family, or friends. As trainers know, timing matters, so develop a plan right now and gather whatever materials you will need. Thank-you cards in your stationery drawer are much easier to send than ones that are still at the store. You might also offer occasional small thank-you gifts—a small gift certificate or token. Be creative here, too—for example, perhaps a local pet supply store or boutique would like the opportunity to supply you with some gift certificates or coupons specifically for your clients, at no cost to you. It could be a nice marketing opportunity for them to bring people into their store. Offering a $5 gift certificate could turn into a much larger sale for them, and maybe even a regular customer. And in return you are developing another marketing relationship that will likely become a source of referrals.

Marketing maxim #14: Engage support

Though it is probably the most important thing you can do for your business, marketing is often the last task on our list, one we often don't get to. Working with dog pros across the country, I've noted several reasons that keep people from marketing their businesses:

- A lack of ideas. Hopefully this chapter has helped you to develop some effective and creative ideas to market your business.

- A lack of time. There's no getting around this one. You have to make the time. The good news is that time well spent now while building or growing your business means strong word-of-mouth later. You might take a look at the section on scheduling in Chapter 8 to get ideas on how to create marketing time for yourself.

- Marketing is scary and intimidating. Dog pros by and large are terrifically competent and intelligent people, so why should marketing be so hard for them? Because, like all humans, we fear rejection. It's uncomfortable to walk into a vet's office and ask for their referrals because they might say no. That is one of the benefits of active marketing:

You don't have to walk in and risk rejection because you aren't asking for anything—you're walking in as a colleague to offer them a valuable service.

- Fear of failure. Most of us carry this with us to some degree. You have to be a risk taker to start a business. I've seen clients find all sorts of ways to drag their heels—revisiting already made decisions, deciding they want a different color scheme than the one already on their cards, "taking a break" until after the holidays or to get ready for the holidays or because they need to find a new accountant or "just have too much going on." For many, the mind creates roadblocks to protect itself from the risk of failure. But no risk, no gain. At some point, you have to take the plunge.

But you don't have to plunge alone. Consider ways you might provide yourself some support as you take on your marketing tasks. Perhaps you can assemble a Think Tank group of colleagues or friends that would be good sounding boards for your ideas. Also set deadlines for yourself— if you've made an appointment with the local shelter to provide then with an adopter's package you'll have to have it done by that date. Look around for classes or seminars geared towards marketing a training business. And consider engaging professional support as well. Working with a business coach can make a huge difference in creating and fleshing out ideas, helping with strategies for making initial contacts with other businesses (including developing language that feels comfortable to you), and carrying out implementation of your marketing plan.

Is it working? Track your marketing success

Marketing maxim #15: Track your ROI

You'll be putting a lot of work and time into your marketing, and probably a bit of money, too. Don't waste either on efforts that don't bring you results. A simple plan for tracking ROI—return on investment—saves time and frustration, so make sure to ask everyone who calls you where they heard about your business and keep track of their answers. Note which callers turned into actual clients—there is no point continuing a marketing strategy that brings in the wrong people. ROI tracking can be a simple matter of keeping a tracking sheet by the phone—you can find a sample in the Resources.

CASE STUDY

At first Kate was delighted by the response to her phone book ad. Yes, it had cost a lot, but the phone sure was ringing! She kept track of the number of calls that came from people seeing the ad—the number was more than she'd dared hoped for. But a few months later Kate wasn't feeling nearly as enthusiastic. Her record keeping revealed that very few of the phone book ad calls were turning into clients! Because she was paying attention, she was able to reassess her ad and decided to put her money and time into a more effective marketing strategy.

Another reason to track ROI is to fend off doubts and discouragement. I often see clients decide that something isn't working when they've simply had a bad week. After examining the data they realize things are coming along well—and the sense of being in control, having one's finger on the pulse of the business, makes them feel better, too.

Lastly, don't forget to give each of your marketing efforts enough time to work—few show an impact right away. People take time to think and make a decision. That's why repeated contacts are a marketing rule. Six months is a minimum before you can reasonably expect to judge the effect of any given strategy or project.

Chapter 5
KEEP THEM COMING BACK

Though it's often a profound love of dogs that brings people to the dog services profession, most dog pros soon catch on that the human client is at the center of the business. The client lives with the dog day and night while we see them in short bursts. And then there's this reality: Dogs don't carry checkbooks and day planners. If we're going to work with dogs, and be paid for our efforts, we have to take good care of their people.

Follow up and keep in touch

Few dreams are more alluring to the small business owner than the one in which a business builds itself by word of mouth. We've all heard some version of the story: Without a marketing budget or any tedious foot-work, Let Sleeping Dogs Lie Inc. grew from a garage outfit to a three-star, nationwide Boarding and Kenneling enterprise. Who wouldn't want that? And yet most business owners sorely neglect even the most basic cultivation of referrals, without a doubt the cheapest and easiest form of marketing available.

Your clients lead busy lives, and people are only capable of focusing on a finite number of things at once. An obvious statement, yes, but if you keep this truth in mind you can make your business and training practices more effective.

Once a client stops actively working with a trainer, his or her commitment to daily training begins to slip—especially when the training has improved a dog's behavior. As trainers we know that old, unwanted behaviors, practiced many more times than the new, will begin to resurface.

When that happens, some owners return to what you taught them and regain lost ground. But many don't have sufficient skill or understanding to do so. Hopefully they'll call you. But some won't. Perhaps they're too busy or believe the training didn't work because the same old problem is back again. Maybe they're embarrassed. Don't count on referrals from these clients. Instead, they're more likely to tell friends, "Well, we hired a trainer and it sort of seemed to work, but then Milo just started up the barking again. I'm not sure what to try next." Clearly not the type of endorsement that will bring you word-of-mouth business.

Dog walkers and daycare operators have a different challenge—your clients get so used to you being in their lives they almost forget you're there, especially if you pick up and drop off their dogs while they're working. These owners may not think to offer referrals because you do your job so well you've dropped below their daily radar.

For sitters, a job well done usually means a return client. But timely check-ins will help clients remember to schedule early for their trips, vacations, and holidays, which is a great help to your scheduling.

Follow-up benefits
Following up with clients regularly is important. If it sounds like extra time, then yes it is, but time spent marketing your business is time spent generating business. And that's how you should think of follow-ups: it should be a standard marketing practice for you. Trainers, some of your clients will be in situations in which they need you to come back for a touch-up. Had you not checked in they might not have gotten around to calling you. Because you called they got the help they needed, are happy with the ongoing results, and are more likely to tell friends and family about you.

For all dog pros, checking in briefly and respectfully with clients will keep you in their line of sight. In Chapter 4, I mentioned the importance of repeat contacts. Regular follow-ups constitute repeat contact with your clients—keeping yourself in their consciousness. Regardless of whether they need help, owners are more likely to refer someone to you if they've had recent contact with you. In other words, if you are part of the finite number of things on their minds. And your consistent concern for them helps build their loyalty.

Use a follow-up system
Decide in advance how often you want to follow up with each client. Trainers might choose to check in after two weeks, 1 month, 3 months, 6 months, 1 year, and then twice a year thereafter. Have a schedule or a

spot on your weekly calendar where you note the dates for each client. Many email programs have functions that will automatically alert you of pre-set dates and tasks. Set aside a few hours once a week at a regular time to take care of all your follow-up calls or emails for the week. Dog walkers might choose to leave a quick note or send an email daily to let dog parents know how much fun their dog had that day. Daycares can send a weekly "report card" home detailing their dog's most notable moments and any new accomplishments. Sitters can also use a post-stay report card as well as checking in with clients a few times a year via email or a card (or another marketing idea such as a newsletter) to remind owners to sign up early for summer vacations and holiday trips.

Practice your follow-up routine efficiently. Have rules about what you will help with over the phone and when you will suggest a follow-up appointment. Unless you want to spend hours on each phone call, avoid general, open questions like "How are things going?" or "How is Toto?" Instead, help clients stay on task by asking specific questions such as, "I wanted to check in on how Toto is doing when he sees other dogs—is he looking at you instead of barking?" And once you've hit the one year mark you can choose to send cards as follow-ups instead of calling—especially if the previous check-ins have been positive. A quick handwritten card is a nice touch and takes less time than a phone call.

Using prompts and positive reinforcement to build referrals

Another obvious but often overlooked practice is to ask for referrals. It is funny how many people don't think to offer them—even when they're happy with a service. Most likely this is another function of how many things vie for our attention in a hectic culture. By simply asking for referrals—and rewarding them—you can make a huge difference for your business.

Prompt them

You don't have to be bold or pushy to ask for a referral. Instead, watch for comfortable opportunities. When a client offers praise such as "Thank you so much—you are great! I can't believe the difference training has made!" this is a perfect time to say "Thank you—I'm so glad I could be of help to you and Clifford, and it's been such a pleasure working with you. I hope you'll let any friends, family, or co-workers with dogs know about your training experience. If you know anyone you think might benefit from training I'd be delighted to work with them as well." They've just told you how wonderful you are, and you're able to slip the request naturally into conversation without any worry of being rejected. And they're more likely to send referrals your way because you've introduced the notion.

Reinforce them

Reinforce every referral, and practice good timing—just like when you train. Use a system to help with efficiency and promptness. Keep a database of client contact information in one place (such as an Excel spreadsheet or professional dog business software), stock up on thank-you cards or postcards (all the better with your business name and logo), and have a variety of thank-you tokens on hand. For example, ask a local pet supply store to provide you with coupons (a marketing opportunity for them, too). And make up coupons for your own services—a small discount off the next training class or next pet sitting, or a free day for dog walking or daycare clients. You can also send small items with your logo on them—small bags of dog treats, for example. Having many ways to say thank you is great for clients who send multiple referrals, as you don't want your gesture of appreciation to look routine.

For clients who consistently send others your way, occasionally (once or twice per year) send a general thank you, not directly related to any particular referral, in which you express your gratitude for their ongoing support and share how much you enjoy working with the people in their lives.

Prompts vs. lures

These suggestions are similar to using prompts and rewards in dog training—analogous, say, to a hand signal followed by a treat. In my experience, it's best to avoid outright lures with clients—offering something up front for a recommendation: "I'll give you such-and-such a discount if you send your friends to me." You may see some success from this approach, but not necessarily any more than from a prompt. Prompts lead to the first referral and your reinforcements keep them coming. This way you build loyalty—your clients suggest you because they believe in you—and that makes for stronger referrals.

It works with your marketing network, too

Finally, why not also use the ideas in this chapter to cultivate referrals from other marketing connections? Other dog professionals and services, and anyone else you are networked with, can be excellent sources of referrals. Just don't forget to return the favor whenever you can.

Chapter 6

THE NUTS AND BOLTS: SERVICES, RATES, AND POLICIES

Many an overworked dog pro leaves the task of defining her services, rates, and policies until the last minute, generally when some unanticipated question or problem arises. Perhaps it occurs when you are faced with a marketing decision such as choosing text for a web site or flyer. Or worse, you have to scramble to come up with an off-the-cuff answer when your first client calls asking a question about how you handle cancellations. It can be embarrassing, because what, after all, should be more self-explanatory than the services of a dog trainer or walker, right? It seems simple, but if there is a lack of clarity about the services you provide and, even more importantly the ones you don't, you leave yourself open to misunderstandings and confusions, perhaps outright conflict. The time spent now defining your services, their costs, and the resultant policies is guaranteed to spare you many future headaches. See the Service Comparison chart in the Resources.

Training services
If you are starting a training business, there are a number of service-related issues you need to clearly define.

1. What training issues do you cover? Do you work on basic obedience, puppy issues, basic behavior problems like impulse control issues, serious issues such as shy or fearful dogs, aggression, or competition training including obedience or sports? Is there a behavior issue or type of training you will not work on? For example, are you comfortable working with aggression? If so, in what forms and

at what severity? Will you work cases with a bite history or with children in the house?

2. What kind of dogs will you work with? Do you have limitations on size or breed or age of the dogs you're willing to take on?

3. What kind of support services will you offer? Will you be available by phone or email to answer follow-up questions? And if so, will you charge for this or build it into your rates? How will you place boundaries around such a support service? Will you offer written homework notes? If so, will you write them on the spot, or type them up and email them?

4. Will you work directly with your human clients or train their dogs for them? Will you train privately or in groups?

Let's look at this last issue in more detail. Your basic options are in-home training, day training, board and train, and public classes.

In-home training

In the last decade this has become a popular format for positive-based trainers. Because positive-based trainers place so much emphasis on changing the way people understand and interact with their dogs, training the people rather than the dogs has become a mantra. Focusing on training the owner has a lot of advantages, chiefly because the training is done in the context of the home and by the client—meaning the dog responds to the owner instead of the trainer. This method of training is more likely to be effective and last for the long haul. Many clients like this method since it usually costs less than board and train situations, and the owner gets to keep his dog with him during the process.

Ideally an owner will learn enough both conceptually and skill-wise to be able to continue working with his dogs on other training goals as well, but the drawback is that it can be a slow process. The reason for this is not, as is sometimes assumed, that positive methods are inherently slow, but rather that it takes a lot of time to train humans. As trainers we are faced with the challenge of trying, typically in one-hour segments once a week, to train people to do the highly skilled work that we ourselves learned over a much longer time period and in much more concentrated doses.

Where basic obedience and puppy raising are concerned, there is much to be gained in return for the time invested. And in-home training is a must for issues that require a behavior modification plan with a large management component, such as digging, chewing, counter surfing, jumping on guests, watch dog barking, housetraining, and separation anxiety. For these problems, teaching the owner to do the training is optimal because the work needs to happen in the context of the dog's everyday life. Coaching clients in their own homes also allows trainers to design plans that take into account the client's routines and environment, thus increasing the likelihood of compliance and success.

But the issue becomes muddled when we consider complicated behavior modification techniques for serious issues. Should we be teaching such techniques to guardians for self-implementation? Lack of essential training skills, consistency, and perseverance on the part of the guardian often lead him or her to give up before any discernable progress has been made. And while a flimsy recall or intermittent sit hurts only the guardian's pride, dog-dog aggression left untreated could have serious consequences. Some behavioral issues are generally best left to the professionals when possible. After all, does a lawyer teach a client how to argue a case himself? Does a doctor teach a patient how to do his or her own operation? Nevertheless, given the higher costs of other options such as board and train and day training, there is often no other choice but to use in-home training for heavier behavioral work.

In-home training is best suited for trainers with highly developed teaching/coaching and interpersonal skills. And clients who enjoy working with their dogs (versus those that "just want the problem solved") and who exhibit strong mechanical skills are likely to thrive with this approach. Many will also prefer it for the lower cost and the convenience of having someone come to their home.

Day training
Day training as a category falls somewhere between in-home training and board and train. The trainer trains the dog in the dog's home, and then teaches the human client the required skills and concepts to maintain the training. One advantage of day training is schedule flexibility, as the training can be done during the day; another, that you often see faster progress than with other methods because a professional trainer can get more done in the same number of hours. Such speedy improvement is in itself thrilling to a guardian and rarely fails to spark a high level of engagement, but compliance often increases too, because the effort required maintaining the training is less than what would be needed for the client to train to that level herself. Finally, your client may appreciate the convenience of having her doggie goals addressed while she's at work. The central disadvantage of day training from a client's perspective is that it typically comes with a larger price tag than in-home training.

Obedience (especially issues that demand more practice time such as leash manners) and long-winded, highly technical problems like fear and aggression lend themselves particularly well to this format.

Day training works best for trainers who enjoy flexible scheduling and lots of hands-on time with dogs. You will still need excellent coaching skills to teach the concepts and mechanics necessary to keep new behaviors strong and/or old behaviors at bay, though many trainers find teaching maintenance easier than coaching behavior modification from the beginning. Partly this is because the level of skill necessary is somewhat less. Much is also likely due to the owner's reduced anxiety levels and the strong buy in that come with seeing the trainer's results. Clients who have less time than money or who require more immediate results may prefer day training.

Board and train

If you are able to house dogs in your own home, board and train can be a very lucrative option. There is a sizeable market segment of people willing and able to pay a premium for the convenience and expediency of having a dog taken away and returned without the behavior problem or with new behaviors ready to go. Of course, one or two appointments at a minimum are required in which you teach the guardian how to maintain the new results in her home. Other benefits of board and train are that you can work with the dog at your own convenience, and that it can be a quicker approach than in-home training and day training, given that you have many more trial opportunities daily than you would if you worked with the dog in its own home.

Board and train works well for obedience, basic manners, and aggression. Like day training, however, it is not as effective for behaviors such as housetraining, destruction, counter surfing etc., for which management in the dog's home environment is a key component of the training plan.

Trainers who enjoy working directly with dogs and who prefer fewer coaching hours can find board and train particularly satisfying. Still, as with day training, teaching skills are crucial for transferring the results from your house to that of your clients. Owners with the available capital who need faster results (or who travel frequently and want to get more from their boarding buck) may appreciate being able to send Fido on over to your place.

Group classes

Classes are great for basic obedience and fun activities such as sports and tricks, and puppy classes are an essential modern component of proper socialization (so long as they are run properly to avoid negative play experiences and opportunities to practice inappropriate social behaviors). On average, however, a class is not necessarily the easiest or most beneficial environment for behavior issues—an exception would be dog-dog reactivity; some places are generating impressive results with Growly Dog (aggression) classes. The time-honored setting of a class appeals to many people, combining, as it does, a relatively inexpensive way to train a dog with a pleasant social activity. Classes also present an opportunity to spread the word about your private services.

Dog walking services

The major questions concern whether to walk dogs on or off leash, individually or in groups. On-leash walking with one dog at a time is the simplest, safest way to go but is also the slowest to generate revenue. Walking a group of dogs off leash together is a better revenue generator, but requires considerable skill and knowledge if it is to be done safely and well.

Another central matter is who you will walk. Will you take a dog with a poor recall? What about those with indecorous car manners? Do you feel safe walking a resource guarder or a dog with human aggression or dog reactivity?

From a marketing standpoint it pays to be absolutely clear about the extras you are planning to offer, if any. For example, what kind of clean up will you provide the dogs—none at all, a rub-down with a towel after a muddy walk, a hosing off in the yard, a bath once a week? Will you carry out any additional tasks, such as feeding or checking water bowl levels, maybe leaving the dogs with a Kong or other stimulation toy?

Dog sitting services

The number one question for sitters is whether to sit in the client's home or in your own. The advantage of your own home is, well, that you get to be home and can maintain much, if not all, of your normal routine, which is particularly important if you have a significant other or a family. The advantage of sitting in the pet's home is that the pet is often more comfortable and relaxed there, and many clients prefer this service—particularly if they have other animals such as fish, rabbits, birds, or reptiles that cannot easily be moved.

Another important service area to define is the precise type and extent of your sitting. Will you be staying overnight in the pet's home or dropping in—and if the latter—for how long exactly? Often a client will pay a premium to know that his or her animal is being kept company overnight but, in addition to being a time-consuming commitment, it also means that you cannot personally take on more than one client at a time.

Are you a pet sitter, a dog and cat sitter, or just a dog sitter—which animals are you comfortable caring for? Do you have the necessary knowledge and skills to, say, feed a reptile or provide mental stimulation for rats or rabbits?

Finally, will you attend to additional tasks such as watering plants (indoors and/or outdoors) and bringing in mail? The advantage is that there are clients who would gladly pay for such comprehensive services while they are away. The downside is that you may feel that such tasks undermine your professional image.

Daycare services

Will you offer just daycare, or will you also board dogs? Boarding can be very lucrative, and you have a well-primed target market at hand in your daycare patrons. On the other hand, it involves camping out overnight at your facility, which you would either have to do yourself or pay a staff member to do. Either way, the costs need to be factored into your overhead.

What other services might you offer to open up new revenue streams for your business? Could you, and do you want to, offer individual training or public classes? Grooming? Retail? Dog massage? Yes, these types of services complicate your business but the more you provide the greater your potential income, and you can more readily compete with other daycares if clients see your business as a one-stop shop for their dog's needs.

To package or not to package?

Packaging a bundle of services and charging less for them than you would on an individual basis can be a very attractive option both for the business owner and the client. An increasing number of dog pros, regardless of the type of services they offer, are finding that packaging is a sound business strategy.

Advantages

For dog trainers, well designed packages can be a three-way win—for you, your client, and the dogs. For you, it means more time doing your actual business and less time spent marketing. So if you don't enjoy being a salesperson and dislike having to sell the next session each time you meet with a client, packaging is a terrific way to lump all the selling into a one-time or, at the very least, an infrequent event. You only have to present the material and convince the potential client once, and then you can get to work. Packaging also means a better chance of receiving longer-term income from each client depending on how you structure the services.

The benefit for the client is that she is more likely to get the help she needs. It sounds basic but is no small boon. So many of life's interventions can get in the way of dog training—money concerns, suddenly getting too busy at work, or getting just enough relief from a problem to decide not to continue (which any trainer will tell you is a situation likely to unravel in the long term). Your client is much more likely to meet her goals if she has committed herself to a certain number of training sessions and has paid for them in advance.

This, in turn, provides you with a better chance of helping the dog. If you see the client (or the dog) enough times to "fix" the problem, the likelihood is that the dog's quality of life is going to improve significantly. The reality is that a well-behaved dog is more popular in its home, and is generally safer in its dealings with the world and from threats of re-homing and euthanasia. Few things are harder for a trainer than knowing you could have helped a client meet her goals but for whatever reason you didn't get the chance to do so, and now falling short of those goals could mean the dog will suffer.

For walkers and daycare operators, packages guarantee regular income and are really a must. A drop-in approach to walking and daycare is messy and inefficient as a business model. You never have an accurate grasp of your monthly income, if pick-up routes are involved they vary daily and require new planning, and your pack composition changes every day. This adds unnecessary work for you and your staff, and is stressful for the dogs. Packages allow you to streamline your operation for the optimum number of lucrative clients, meaning you avoid the risk of having to turn someone away because you're too full. Best to spare yourself the aggravation of having to say no to someone who wants regular care five days a week because you have too many twice-a-week dogs on Thursdays.

Disadvantages

Some dog pros eschew packages because the process of having to make a large sale at the outset of a client relationship is downright torturous to them. And sure, some clients may outright refuse to commit a chunk of funds and time right away. Ultimately it is up to you. Can you overcome any squeamishness about salesmanship for the higher good of your business? Or is it just too far outside your comfort zone? If so, it is certainly possible to run a successful dog pro business without ever offering a package. And I've heard a few dog pros say they prefer the positive reinforcement of being paid at each session. But if you believe, as I do, that packages are the way to go, you have to decide whether or not to take clients who don't want them. Some dog pros opt to do both, while others choose to work only with clients willing and able to make the greater commitment. Naturally, there's room for both types of businesses.

When and how to sell a package

An example of an effective way to offer a package and one-off deal combination could be a walker/sitter who sells off-leash outings in package format only, but complements this service with on-leash walks on an as-needed basis for existing clients or as part of her sitting services. A trainer, on the other hand, might offer a choice of either week-to-week commitment or longer-term packages for obedience work, while insisting on packages for behavior modification.

With obedience packages, program length is less of a concern and a client can happily choose whatever option she can afford. After all, it is a fairly simple matter of how many obedience cues will be learned and some guardians attain the skills quicker than others. But where addressing a serious behavior issue such as resource guarding or stranger fear is concerned, it rarely makes sense to allow the client to choose the number of sessions herself. You, as the expert, know what needs to be done and can determine the amount of time needed. If you allow a client to choose a three session package for something you know will take at least six, you are setting everyone up for failure—yourself, the client, and the dog. Needless to say this doesn't make for good business, as your chances of building a strong referral base dwindle if you are not finishing cases.

So if behavior issues form part of your service menu, it is worth spending some time developing language that explains your package policy. Something along the lines of: "I would be very happy to help you with Roxie's fear of people. We should be able to make significant improvements, but stranger fear is a complex behavioral issue that takes time to address. To help you meet your goals, we will need (insert number here) sessions. Now, I require my clients to commit to the whole behavior modification program because I see too many people get part way to a result and then get pulled away by other commitments. I want to see you meet your goals for Roxie, and I know this is the time it will take. I recognize that this is a large commitment, and so will put a package together for you with a discount off my regular hourly fee. If you'd like to get started I have an opening next week…"

The idea here is that you are granting a discount (it doesn't have to be large—even $5 off each hour is helpful and can make a client feel like he is making a saving) to offset the commitment of the package, but the clear implication is that without a package there'll be no training. And the language centers on the client's needs and your desire and ability to help. Some clients will choose not to pay. That is okay. As you know if you're already in this business, you don't get everyone. But you are more likely to make money and enjoy your business if you work with people who are truly committed. The client is more likely to reach her goals, which means you feel good and so does the client, and she might even want to tell her friends about you. It is a rare client who offers a referral to a service from which she didn't see a result.

As for selling a package, I recommend an initial consult with a new client first. Let them meet you and gain confidence and trust in your abilities before you suggest the financial and durative commitment of a package. With a complete interview and a chance to meet the dog and the guardian you'll also have a better idea of what package is most appropriate.

How to design a package

Walking and daycare packages are usually monthly affairs. You set a price for the month based on a daily rate.

As mentioned above, dog trainers do well to treat obedience and behavior issues separately. For obedience, you might offer a number of package sizes, and I recommend spending some time finding inviting or fun names, too; it helps with the marketing later on. You might also describe roughly the number of things that can be accomplished in each. For some of my clients we have designed a chart where people can choose a certain number of behaviors from one or another box depending on the size of the package.

For behavior problems, you must obviously pinpoint the number of sessions based on what you learn in the initial client interview. What are the issues, how much time does the client have to work with the dog and how skilled does he or she seem, does the dog appear to be a fast learner or not? Choose a number you think will give you sufficient time to help the client reach his goal without jeopardizing safety and allowing for one or two training glitches along the way. You have to be honest, though; make sure you mention that there are no guarantees and that the guardian's success or lack thereof depends largely on his own efforts.

To keep things simple you might have two package prices in mind, both based on an hourly fee. For example, let's say your regular hourly fee is $100. Perhaps you charge $95 an hour for behavior packages of five sessions and under and $90 an hour for packages of six or more sessions. So an eight session package would be 8 x $90=$720 (without a package discount, it would be $800). If you worry about doing math on the spot, have a little chart in your briefcase or pack that you can refer to. I don't recommend posting these prices—simply give each client the price and discount as you explain your services. You can advertise the availability of discount packages on your website and other materials with a general statement if you'd like but package session and price details are best avoided. This is partly because you don't want clients to have the impression that package size is up to them. And partly because many people who may not have called due to pricing might, once they talk with you, be happy to pay your fees. There is a counter argument to this advice, however. If you are profoundly uncomfortable discussing money with potential clients, placing all prices on your site means that most owners who call have already decided that your fees are acceptable to them, reducing that aspect of your sales stress.

Another terrific way to sell your services is to design specialized packages, like a puppy package or a new dog package. With a puppy package, for example, you would include time for all the things you think need to be covered with a new puppy owner, including essential knowledge (for example how dogs think and learn), preventative measures (bite inhibition, socialization, handling), immediate needs (such as housetraining), and obedience behaviors. Figure out the number of sessions needed and price it based on a small discount from your regular hourly fee. If you specialize in something, think about how you might dress that specialization up in a package.

CASE STUDIES

Suzanne, a dog trainer, saw many clients just once or twice, and this transient state of affairs was not only disappointing, it made running her business that much harder. Together we went through a sample of her past cases and identified a pattern—clients who stayed on for just enough help to smooth over whichever troubling dog behavior had caused them to contact Suzanne in the first place, and then, after experiencing some modest relief, chose not to continue with additional sessions. All the while Suzanne knew she could offer much more, and that in all probability the behavior would resurface fully without additional work. To solve the problem we designed a selection of behavior packages aimed at the types of problems Suzanne saw most often. This or that package, she would explain to a potential client, was designed specifically for the type of problem he or she was faced with and, lo and behold, had an inviting discount built in as well. After several months of working with packages—getting used to selling them and so on—Suzanne saw the majority of her cases follow a healthy and predictably successful pattern, and as a result her client referrals began to climb, too.

Another dog trainer, Kip, was slowly souring on his chosen business. Every weekday evening and all through the weekend when his 9-5 friends were out and about enjoying themselves, Kip was hard at work. And that might have been all right if his clients weren't so universally resistant to completing homework assignments so that progress was slow and hard-won, particularly with behavioral issues. Rather than switching careers, he decided to switch his former one-on-one in-home training practice to owner-absent day training packages. Training dogs primarily during the day left more time open to see friends and the few hours now needed to coach a client on maintenance skills was much easier and more fulfilling for Kip than teaching him or her to train from scratch. Some clients opted to leave when Kip's services changed, but the majority responded with previously unseen enthusiasm for the maintenance work because they had seen such swift changes in their dogs.

What do you charge? Setting your rates

Setting rates is relatively simple and yet in my experience many dog pros find the process stressful. What it boils down to is this: in much of mainstream America, dog training, walking, sitting, and other canine services have traditionally been regarded with bemused indulgence and even low-level disdain. And to be fair, the industry has attracted and nurtured its share of eccentrics over the years, many of whom had no formal education or experience. The stubborn stereotype—of the unschooled, self-taught, largely anti-social dog trainer—and the widespread misconception that dog walking or sitting requires no skills whatsoever may be alive and well in places, but they are wholly untrue, and every dog pro owes it to him or herself to contribute to their annihilation. In the face of this, the challenge for most business owners is believing that they can demand a good rate and that they are worth it. Well, there really is no other way for me to say this than: You are. Your services are valuable, in fact they are essential. At present, there are roughly 68 million pet dogs in America and that number is growing steadily. Without having to get into the tragic figures of dogs that are given up, re-homed, or euthanized every year due to common and highly treatable behavior issues, suffice it to say that dogs and their guardians need you. By all means charge for your professional knowledge and skill set.

To set your rates, first look at your competition. You can start with an internet search for like businesses and then call them for additional information if needed, or ask a friend to do so if you prefer. If you are fortunate enough not to have any local competition, examine the competition in an area similar to your own in terms of human, canine, and economic demographics. What are they charging? And what do they offer for those fees? How is the service similar to or different from what you plan to offer or are offering? Come up with three numbers—the lowest anyone is charging, the highest, and the average.

Now look at your income needs. What is the bottom line of revenue you need to live on? How many clients would you need to have at the average local rate and at the highest local rate? Analyze this until you have a good grasp of the numbers involved.

Next, consider what your time and skills feel worth to you. Imagine yourself completing a training session or finishing a walk or a sitting appointment. Imagine the client handing you a check. Look down at the figure on the check (once you're in the car of course, not in front of the client!). It's the lowest number in your area. How does that feel? Look down again. It's the average price for your area. What does your gut say? Look one more time at the highest price paid in your area. What do you think?

Don't forget your intended audience—who are your potential clients? Are you drawing from a wealthy neighborhood, middle class suburb, or working class area?

Finally, give some thought to marketing—where on the bell curve does it make sense for your business to sit? At the bottom end, up in front, with the pack, or somewhere in between the pack and the leader? Yes, you may get more calls if you're priced low. But do you want your clients to be bargain hunters or committed guardians? Many people find that clients who pay less have lower compliance and/or do not value the service provided them as highly. If you're priced in the middle, be sure to have something else that sets you apart from everyone else in the same spot (see the Niche section of Chapter 4). The psychology of charging at the top is underpinned by the widely held American beliefs that "you get what you pay for" and that cost equates quality. And don't forget your overall marketing message—if what makes you special in your area, for example, is being the only certified dog pro, then it wouldn't make sense to charge at the lower end.

Consider all these factors and make a decision. Be especially careful on two counts. One, don't undersell yourself. Again, your services are valuable and worth paying for. Two, set your regular fee high enough so that when you factor in discounts you are still being paid what you want to make.

Can we reschedule? Setting effective policies, or training your clients

Having strong policies that you scrupulously enforce actively trains your clients to behave as you wish them to, and in the long run this strategy reduces the risk of conflict, saves untold amounts of exasperation, and protects your revenue. In summary, the sooner you attack this task the better.

Cancellation and vacation policies

Contrary to what we all might wish, the tricky area of cancellations can seldom be addressed with a laid-back attitude, because the consequences of last-minute or frequent cancellations deeply affects your revenue as well as your effectiveness.

This is hardest for trainers. If you use a package and the client cancels or is a no-show, he has already paid for the missed session. But if you don't reschedule, you cannot help him or his dog. At the same time you can't very well allow your schedule to fill up with missed appointments when you could have filled those slots training additional clients. If you work session to session you have the option of charging them and rescheduling, though in my experience few trainers are comfortable doing that. Some trainers try to get around the issue by implementing a compliance policy. They express to the client the importance of his getting to sessions and explain that other people could use those spaces and that cancellations are not acceptable except for illness and emergencies. They then set a number of cancellations (should be a low number, perhaps two) that result in a forfeiture of training, with no refund for any missed or already used sessions.

It is my recommendation for walkers and daycare operators that you require clients to be full time, five-day-a-week clients, and that you invoice in advance for the month ahead. Your cancellation policy should be strict, as the lost income from any cancellation—even one with reasonable notice—cannot really be replaced. Present it to your clients this way: they are paying for a spot for their dog, whether they use it or not. It's like paying for a spot for a child in daycare—you may choose to keep your child home on a given day or for a week to visit grandma, but the daycare does not give you a credit for this. You pay for the entire month whether you use it or not, because you are paying for the privilege of the spot. Gym membership is another analogy—you pay monthly for the ability to go each day. If you only go two days a week or even if you never show up you still pay for the full month. This way you can build a business with a reliable income. A few clients may balk at this idea, but again, why not work with those who understand that your services are worth what you charge?

The above is a so-called no cancellation policy, which requires notification of an absence but grants no compensation. Another option is to give your clients a set amount of time off, such as two weeks (ten days) per year. In this scenario, if a client gives you notice the month before invoices can be adjusted to reflect the coming month's absence. After he has used up his ten days, notice is still required, but the client pays in full. Some dog pros like this approach for the flexibility it affords the client, a clear benefit to herald when marketing. Others find the adjusting of invoices a hassle and do not allow compensation for any absences.

Sitters might consider using a graduated cancellation policy based on the amount of notice given. For example, if someone gives you a month's notice, is that enough time to fill the space? If so, you might offer a full refund for cancellations a month in advance. As you get closer to the sitting dates, the amount of refund diminishes. Perhaps you give a 50% refund with two weeks notice, and no refund with shorter notice. There is no correct answer here—you have to look at the likelihood of filling the space and set your policy accordingly.

Homework and compliance policies

Trainers differ greatly in their approach to homework compliance. Flexibility on this often sensitive subject may gain you longer-term business and loyalty from busy or overwhelmed clients. The drawback, however, is your own risk of burnout, as it can be intensely frustrating to see time pass with hardly any progress made. And there are trainers out there who swear by the strictest of homework policies—if you don't do it, you're fired. It comes down to personal preference, and all I generally recommend is that you think the matter over carefully, decide where you stand, and then clearly communicate your expectations to your clients at the outset of the relationship.

Aggression cases are a notable exception. Here, an ironclad homework policy can save lives and protect your business, and any trainer who takes on aggression ought to have such a policy. Say, for example, you are working with a dog that has a history of biting, and you recommend that the dog be muzzled in public. Well, then you can't leave it to the guardian to decide whether or not she feels like complying on any given day, you must insist she does, because if she is neglecting her muzzle desensitization work and/or is taking the dog outside, people are at risk, the dog's life is at risk, and your own personal liability is much higher.

When a client consistently struggles to complete their homework, ask yourself first if your training plan can be adjusted to better suit their lifestyle and skills. If you've done all you can on that front, think about switching them to day training or board and train if doing so would be appropriate for their training goals and within their budget.

A note on this for walkers and daycare operators: if you decide to ask a client to take care of a behavior issue be sure to give him or her a specific timeframe in which it must be done, and be clear about any consequences of not following through.

Payment policies

I always advise my clients to ask for payment prior to the rendering of services, with the exception of initial training consults, which are paid at the time of the consult. It is just sound business. It cuts down on repeated cancellations, it secures a consistent stream of revenue, and it is the only way to project income with any kind of certainty, something which is required if you ever wish to expand your business, branch into new areas, save for your retirement, or hire employees. Again, when presenting your payment policy to your clients, make it clear that their outlay reserves a space—whether in a walking group or in a daycare or in your sitting or training schedule.

Communicating and enforcing policies

Whatever policies you end up choosing, communicate them to your clients in a frank and straightforward manner. Policies should be written in your contract and you should explain them verbally as well. It also helps to have the client initial the policy section of the contract so there is no chance of hearing, "Well, I didn't know."

Be clear in your mind about what action you will take if a client breaks a policy. Will you give a one-time warning, or will you enact the policy on the first infringement? If you feel that it is reasonable to give a warning, only give one and make it very clear. Say a new client cancels a dog sitting appointment. You might say, "I'm sorry to hear that Bailey won't be with us next weekend. As you know, our policy is not to give refunds without a two week notice. Since you are new to us, I'm going to refund the sitting fee minus a processing charge just this time."

Changing your rates and policies

If you are reading this chapter and fretting over a lack of policies or real-izing that your rates are too low, don't worry. You can make changes, even large ones. The key to smoothly changing rates or policies is to give your clients plenty of notice. Depending on the size of the change, you might give them several months.

Communicate the change in writing first, and yes, use old-fashioned pa-per and envelopes. Then follow up at least a couple of times, either by email or in person, and finally provide a reminder close to the date of the change.

In the initial letter, explain the change clearly and, if appropriate, the rea-sons behind it. Avoid the inclination to over-apologize or over-explain. If you worry that the change may result in some clients leaving your servic-es, ask them early on to communicate their intentions to you. You may be surprised just how few clients choose the door. If you've done your job well a small inconvenience will not shake their loyalty. If you do lose a few clients, you will still benefit in the long run from being paid what you're worth and having clients who respect your policies.

It's a good idea in general to communicate with clients by letter periodi-cally. Have a regular routine of communication so that bad news isn't the only time they hear from you in writing—don't accidentally condition a negative CER (an unpleasant emotional response)—to hearing from you! This also allows you to have a regular routine for announcing changes or updates, which means that you will more easily be able to make rate changes every couple of years in accordance with the economy.

CASE STUDIES

Candy's dog walking rates were low for the area, but she had not raised her rates in years and worried about doing so now. How would she explain the change to her long-standing, loyal clients? Would they balk and go elsewhere? After doing the math, how-ever, she knew she couldn't continue to put it off, and togeth-er we drafted a cheerful letter to her clients about how much she enjoyed their dogs. She explained the change and the rea-sons for it—to bring her rates in line with the current industry average and to cover rising gas costs—and said that she hoped the increase would not prove too much of a burden or inconve-nience. In the end, she was overwhelmed by the response. Many of her clients emailed or called to say that they couldn't imag-ine their dogs' lives without her. Only one client chose to leave, and Candy realized how relieved she was—this had been her one troublesome client, always complaining about money and minute details. She soon had a new client in his place, along with a renewed sense of her work's value and a larger monthly deposit for the bank.

Judy moved across the country to take over a house and kennel that she and her husband had bought to realize their dream of a quiet rural life. Her first morning in their new home, Judy watched in disbelief through the window as a truck pulled up to the kennels and a man got out and left his dog in a run, then drove off without a word. Anxious, she called the previous owner, only to find out that this casual drop-off method was par for the course—all her clients simply stopped by with a dog on a loose as-needed basis. Judy realized in that moment that taking over an existing business would not be as simple as she had hoped. After carefully drafting her policies, Judy wrote a gracious letter introducing herself to the kennel clientele. She presented the new business, including a fresh menu of services with clearly defined kennel policies, and explained the various benefits of her newfangled ways, primarily that her policies would allow her to provide the best care possible for everyone's dogs. She was happy to find that the majority of the customers were willing to comply, and that her innovative and structured way of running things began to pull people in from the nearby towns as well.

Edward specialized in separation anxiety and his training business was booming. This might have been great except that Edward rarely had a moment to stop and breathe, and strongly felt something had to change. An analysis of how he spent his time quickly revealed that far too many of his hours were eaten up by phone conversations and email replies to clients currently working on separation anxiety protocols—all without pay. The amount of money Edward was losing by not charging for this time was staggering. But what to do? His clients needed regular help and support to be successful. We retooled his separation anxiety package to include a pre-determined amount of support time, based on the average client's needs, and built that time into his package price. From then on, Edward informed clients that additional time would be charged separately, and also suggested guidelines for which issues and topics were best handled with follow-up support and which were better suited to in-person work. With this change in policy, and some reworking of his schedule, Edward was soon enjoying his work again—and being paid handsomely for it.

Chapter 7

OLD DOGS: GROWING PAINS

If you have been operating a dog business successfully for a period of time, you are to be congratulated, especially if you're turning a profit. That said, while not all dog businesses develop the same way, many owners experience growing pains as the business matures. Growing pains tend to occur at several key points in the development of a dog-oriented business:

• When business is picking up, but you're still working another job as well.

• When the business has grown to such an extent that the need for better organization and efficiency becomes critical.

• When, because business is booming or because you have a need to increase revenue streams, you're faced with the decision of whether and how to expand.

• When the business is large enough that you need bring in extra help—to take on employees, independent contractors, or partners.

I quit!—Moving from part to full time

Leaving the security of a regular paycheck so you can devote yourself to a full time dog business is often the first critical point as your business matures. Even if that paycheck came with mind-numbing 9-5 boredom, walking away from that security can be both terrifying and exhilarating.

When, for example, is it the right time to make the move? How do you know you'll be safe? There are no one-size-fits-all answers to these questions, and certainly there are no guarantees in the volatile world of self-employment, but careful planning will increase your chances of success and could, if you are anything like me, considerably lower your anxiety levels during the transition period.

Some people are at an advantage because they have supporting income from a significant other, savings, or another source. If that is you, use it. Your business will be up and running faster if you can devote your full energy to its creation and marketing.

But without such luxury you will need a transition plan and the first step is to assess your situation. How much do you make at your job, for how many hours of work? Would you be allowed to pull out of your job gradually by going part time, or is it an all-or-nothing situation? Look at your personal requirements. How much money do you actually need to live on? Now take stock of your business. Based on the rates you charge or plan to charge, how many clients will it take on a regular basis to cover your financial needs? How many clients to fully replace your job income? Are you comfortable leaving your job once your business is making the bare minimum for you to get by on, or do you need it to replace your full job income?

When you have answers to these questions in hand, you are prepared to set transition benchmarks or milestones. You can set benchmarks in terms of money or number of clients. For example, say your goal is to replace your job salary of $30,000 per year, and that your boss says you can go part time to 20 hours when you're ready. This means that your first benchmark will be your business covering $15,000 gross yearly income, or $1,250 per month after business expenses.

To determine your monthly business income, subtract anything you spent on the business from the total you made for the month. Be sure to also subtract 1/12 of any yearly costs. For example, if you use your car for your business and spend an average of $1,500 per year on maintenance, your monthly car expense is $125—$1,500 divided by 12.

So once your business is consistently yielding $1,250 per month (at least three months in a row), request a reduction to 20 hours per week. Your second and final transition milestone is to put in your two weeks notice when your business is consistently bringing in $2,500 per month after expenses. That way you know what you're shooting for, and you know when it's time to leave the job. No more guesswork or worrying.

A word on taxes

Unless you have arranged otherwise through LLC status or incorporation to adjust your tax status, don't forget to adjust your figures by 15% to account for self-employment taxes. For example, to replace $1,250 in work income a business would need to be making $1,437.50 per month, because 15% of $1,250 is $187.50. Consider discussing tax options with a qualified tax accountant—one who has had experience guiding small businesses of all entity types, including sole proprietorships, LLCs, and S Corporations.

CASE STUDIES

Tracy had been transitioning into self-employment for a while, and the effects were taking their toll: dark circles under her eyes, a feeling of being overwhelmed, near-constant worry she'd forgotten something, and a growing strain on her relationship as her husband became increasingly resentful of the evenings and weekends she spent with her clients. But her old employer wasn't willing to let her work part time, and her training revenue could not yet cover her income. She needed a plan to get her through to the other side, and together we devised a clear schedule and marketing plan. She then explained her goals and plans to her husband who, relieved to see a light at the end of the tunnel, agreed to bear down and support her through it. She launched her marketing plan and, six months later, hit her milestone— for three months the business had made the same amount of income as her job. She gave notice and used the new time to reconnect with her husband and implement the larger of her marketing projects. She greatly enjoys working for herself and the reputation she has built as the go-to trainer in the area for serious behavior issues.

In contrast, Donna's transition was fast. Having taught classes for a large pet store chain for several years, she was aching to start her own business offering classes and private training out of her large converted garage. After we crunched the numbers to check the feasibility of starting her own training business, it was clear that a very modest number of clients would replace the income she was making at her job, and an assessment of her savings suggested that she could get up to that baseline while living on what she'd put away. Once we designed her business and marketing plan, Donna quit her job and launched her new business. Her income now comfortably exceeds that from her previous job and she loves training on her own.

Paul's training business had grown as far as it could while he continued to work full time. It had been a slow, organic process based on word of mouth, just a couple clients a week and two weekend classes, but now he was ready to finally take a step toward his dream of training full time. He executed the first two projects of a thoroughly designed marketing plan, and the phone began ringing more often. Once he hit his benchmark number of clients per week he took the leap, scaled his job back to 20 hours to accommodate the new client load and additional time for marketing. Six months later he'd hit his ultimate milestone—the client load goal that indicated it was time to quit his job altogether. Nervous but excited, Paul gave notice and launched the next phase of his marketing plan. He now runs a well-regarded and successful training business.

Managing the transition

Managing the transition to becoming a full time business owner takes forethought and perseverance. Sometimes everything goes perfectly, but usually there is a period of time where you're juggling more than feels comfortable.

For one thing, you likely only have limited outside financial support options, which means that your business will have to cover whatever your financial needs might be—whether that's replacing a previous job's income or reaching a bare minimum number for you to live on. You may have to take a cut in income and lifestyle for a while. It also means you may have some amount of time where you are working full time for a paycheck and devoting your free time to your business—both to handle clients and do your development and marketing. The longer you stay in this transition period, the less likely you are to make it to the other side—it simply gets exhausting, and when you are tired it's easy to become discouraged.

Here are some tips for managing your transition:

Stay focused. Keep the big picture in front of you. At the end of a long day when you're working a job, taking care of yourself and possibly a family, and trying to start your business, questions like "Why am I doing this?" can ring in your ears. Have the answer ready—that you're doing this to improve your quality of life, and when you reach the other side of the transition you'll be doing something you love for a living, and doing it on your own terms. Find whatever motivates you, and make it your mantra. Chant it to yourself whenever you begin to doubt your direction.

Make sacrifices consciously. If you are going to start a business while working, something will have to give. You probably can't do everything you already do and add this large project on top. Make conscious decisions at the outset about what you are willing to temporarily give up to make room for the business. If you don't make this decision things will still fall by the wayside as they are bound to, and you may end up feeling like your quality of life is slipping through your fingers, whereas being realistic and prepared gives you a sense of being in control.

Set and schedule specific goals. Starting a business involves many decisions and tasks that will keep you very busy during the transition period. Without specific goals set out on a timeline, it's much easier to let certain tasks slip, keeping you in transition longer than necessary. Don't fall in this trap. Set goals for each month, and each week (especially for marketing!) and then place those goals into a schedule. Literally decide which blocks of time you will use to accomplish which tasks. If you know you will have two hours on Monday night and two on Wednesday and four hours on Saturday, decide in advance exactly what you will work on during each of those times. This will help you to use the limited time you have as effectively as possible.

Take good care of yourself. Transition can be a stressful and demanding time. Make sure you leave solid chunks of time in your schedule for personal activities that relax and stimulate you. You're much less likely to burnout before you reach your goals if you're feeling physically and mentally your best.

Ask for help. This is the time to rely on friends and family. Get them involved in this exciting phase of your business by asking them for help with specific tasks, or by asking them to take up slack in other areas while you focus on the business. Perhaps they can lend support with babysitting or food sharing or errands. Also consider seeking professional help with your transition. A business support coach or mentor can provide guidance and help you to move through this period as quickly as possible. For more ideas, see the Resources at the back of this book.

There's never a good time to be inefficient and disorganized

Yes, if you have five dog walking clients or teach just one puppy class a week, you can probably get away without being all that streamlined in your operations. But the moment you begin to grow and attract more clients, you'll encounter problems trying to keep up with that growth. At some point in time, nearly all businesses find themselves operating with systems designed for a smaller workload. In other words, what used to work for you no longer does. That's only natural as most of us prefer to concentrate on what we love—working with dogs—rather than updating our systems. But a good, hard look at your systems and how you operate, followed by the appropriate changes, is the cornerstone of business success.

So, when you find yourself in this position, it's time to pause and recreate, otherwise you are sacrificing efficiency and suffering needless stress. Consider Adam from Chapter 1 whose dog walking business was taking him for a walk. Taking clients from various parts of town and allowing them different numbers of days per week worked all right in the beginning, but once his business picked up, the way he was working before was no longer feasible. Adam had to rethink his client strategy, and then put changes into place. If you find your business hindered by inefficiencies, you too should stop and reassess.

Start by clearly identifying the problem. What exactly is causing you to feel harried or stressed? What is causing the inefficiency? Now imagine what things would look like ideally. Adam, for example, wanted to minimize driving time, phone time, and pack management difficulties. Adam wanted his walkers to be able to pick up dogs within a neighborhood. He no longer wanted to field dozens of daily phone calls about whether a particular dog would or would not be walking the next day, and he wanted his walkers to walk the same dogs everyday so that they could gel as a group. The next step was to devise a game plan for implementing these changes. For Adam this meant drafting the new policies (in his case, full-time five-day-per-week clients only and no refunds for cancellations), discussing them with his walkers, and writing a letter to his clients. He set a deadline by which the changes would be made and a deadline by which clients had to notify him if they would no longer be using his services. Once he knew who was staying on board he assigned dogs to walkers based on geography and pack management guidelines (temperament, age, size, etc.). Any clients being assigned a different walker were introduced to the new service provider, walkers took newly assigned dogs out for practice runs, keys were reassigned, and by the deadline everyone was walking packs designed for efficiency.

This process took some additional effort and time, but once implemented made everyone's lives easier. When you feel overwhelmed, the idea of stopping to take stock and then pursue a fix-it project seems impossible, but you must. The worst thing you can do is to keep running. Problems rarely fix themselves. In very extreme cases I've had clients actually close their businesses for a short period (for example, not schedule any clients for a week) in order to make the space needed to carry out an adjustment. If you can't imagine how to fix a problem or carry out a change, get some support assistance. Though it's sometimes hard to see a solution when you're in the middle of a crisis, one nearly always exists.

When to expand and when to stay put

Expansion seems like an obvious goal for most business owners, but it is not always the best decision for everyone. Before you turn your successful private training business into a training center, or a thriving pet sitting business into a daycare, or hire walkers to take out additional packs, think it over carefully. Do you really want this new type of business? I ask the question because if you enjoy what you're doing now it would be a shame to move onto something you don't. Owning a business that exists in real space and has set office hours and overhead is not the same thing as owning a relatively simple home-based operation. So take a moment to really think through what a day in your new life will be like. Ask others who are doing it for some insight—how do they spend an average day? What do they most like? What do they most dislike? What has been most surprising?

And don't be afraid to scale back if your expansion doesn't suit you. If you feel you would enjoy a simpler life again, either hire someone to run the business (or aspects of it that you find challenging or burdensome), sell off part of your business if appropriate, or just scale back what you offer. A central purpose of owning a business, after all, is to better enjoy life.

CASE STUDY

After his first year in business, John's two walking packs were full but he continued to receive calls from potential clients. At first he explained that he was fully booked and simply took down contact information in case of an opening, but it seemed a shame to turn away business. So John hired a walker and, once this person's pack was full, hired another. Soon he had three walkers working for him. At first he reveled in his success, but it didn't take long before he realized he was no longer enjoying his business. The stress of the additional paperwork, scheduling, and responsibility of looking after employees—especially when someone called in sick and his or her walks had to be covered—ultimately didn't feel worth the extra money. John considered his options and decided to go back to what had worked. He sold the extra clients to one of his former employees and now John enjoys two walks a day—again.

Plan ahead

If you decide you would like to expand, have a plan. First, research the costs involved, both one-time up front costs (such as building a space or expanding the use of one you already have) and the ongoing monthly costs. A good real estate agent who handles commercial leases can help you figure space costs if that is part of your plan. Also determine the expense of contractors, your own labor, employees, marketing, and ongoing materials (such as office supplies, training supplies, food and toys, and whatever else you may need). Project your income based on the rates you will charge and a reasonable number of clients. It's a good rule of thumb to inflate costs and be modest about revenue—this creates a safe margin for error. In other words, go with the high end of your cost estimates and the low end of your revenue projections.

Compare these numbers to your current income and savings. Will you have enough money to proceed yourself, or will you need to borrow? If you need financial assistance, the next step is to research your options. Small business loan? Investors? Help from friends or family?

Another decision is whether to expand all at once or in steps. Say you want to open a comprehensive dog services facility. One option is to go for it—open a large facility that offers a variety of services and has a full staff. The main advantage to this approach is in the marketing—you are able to tout yourself as a one-stop shop from the beginning. It may also afford you the opportunity to corner a market if there's one available. Another approach, which is financially less risky, is to figure out which services will be most lucrative and begin with those on a smaller scale, with a plan to expand step by step as revenue allows. In this scenario, the initial offerings raise funds to add or widen a service, which then brings in additional resources to further develop the business, and so on. This could mean leasing a building but only utilizing part of it, or leasing a small building and moving to a larger one as needed. Buying is also an option, but unless you have a surplus of money and the real estate market is just right for it, it's often advisable to start your business life as a renter. Simply put, you're better able to choose the exact right space for your purpose after you've run your business for a number of months or years.

A full-scale business expansion is a complicated endeavor, the details of which are unique to each person's situation and geography, and so cannot be fully sketched out here. If you are contemplating launching such a project, you might benefit from professional support and guidance to help you reach your goals. Visit the Resources at the back of this book.

CASE STUDY

The daycare was nearing Tanisha's full capacity goal. It had been an exciting first year and a half, and Tanisha was proud of herself for starting her business without going into debt. Her next goal was to add boarding. She had the physical space for it in her facility, which is housed in a large warehouse, but it required new construction and the cost to cover it meant getting a loan. Because Tanisha was uncomfortable with that prospect, we devised a gradual expansion plan. Once she hit full daycare capacity, she took some net revenue and used it to build space for boarding two dogs. With the new revenue from the two boarding spaces she builds a third space, and so on, until she had her boarding space fully developed. Her next plan is to add a training room using income from boarding.

Employees, Independent Contractors, and Partners

One sure sign of success is the moment you realize you can no longer carry the work load on your own. If you make the decision to expand, you will need more bodies. Bringing in additional help allows you to grow your business, not only because you can accommodate an increased clientele, but more importantly because it provides you the ability to delegate. And that means more time to focus on what you do best, and more time to devote to growing, marketing, and nurturing your business. You have a number of options—hiring employees, hiring independent contractors, and bringing in a partner are most common—and choosing which path to take is a critical decision with many potential consequences.

Employees

The central advantage of using employees as a means of expansion is control. Unlike independent contractors and partners, you can tell an employee what to do and exactly how to do it. The downside is, of course, that it also increases your paperwork, adds the time and potential stress of management responsibilities, and creates additional expense.

Simply put, an employee is someone hired to work at a company. That person is paid an hourly wage or salary depending on the position, and the employer pays payroll taxes on the money paid to the employee, carries workman's compensation insurance, and must comply with federal and state workplace standards. The employer has full control over the employee—how she does her job, where and when she performs it, what materials she uses, etc. Employers may or may not offer health and other benefits.

Be prepared to spend time training your employees. While it is easy to tell someone what to do, it's important that they know exactly how you want them to do it. Better yet, involve employees in brainstorming and decision making to encourage a higher level of initiative. Good coaching and motivational skills are key to being a good employer and getting the most from your workers. Building a respectful, fun workplace is paramount, and doing so builds loyalty, which may lower your turnover rate.

But beware the additional costs and hassles of being an employer. There is a significant amount of paperwork and cost involved in complying with governmental, labor, and payroll requirements. Becoming an employer is a big step to take and before you make the leap you should calculate all the costs—monetary and time—and compare them to the potential increase in revenue.

Independent Contractors

One alternative to hiring employees is to utilize independent contractors. Properly used, an independent contractor can bring most of the benefits that an employee does but with far less hassle and cost. This is an often-misunderstood topic; so first, let's define what an independent contractor is.

An independent contractor (IC) is a person who owns his or her own business and contracts out time and services to another business. An independent contractor does not work for one employer only—he may contract himself out to multiple employers, and may also offer his own services directly to the public. An IC pays his own employment taxes (the so-called self employment tax) and is responsible for his own insurance and medical coverage. You should, however, supply all independent contractors you used during the year with a 1099 form reporting whatever you paid them for their services. This is a simple procedure, your tax accountant or the IRS can give you assistance if necessary.

An IC schedules his own time and uses his own materials to carry out his work. Of course, if a contract calls for an IC to teach a public class at a certain time, for example, he has to teach it at that time. But he agreed to that, rather than it being dictated to him. An IC is not trained by the people who hire him.

I often hear dog pros talk about hiring sub contractors when, really, they are referring to independent contractors. A sub contractor is someone hired by an IC. A common example is when a building contractor is hired by someone to build a structure. That contractor will most likely turn around and hire an electrician and a plumber to carry out installation of those building features. The electrician and plumber would be sub contractors. You don't see much sub contracting in the dog services industry.

Generally it is to your financial advantage to hire independent contractors if you can. Hiring employees is much more expensive—you have the payroll taxes, workman's compensation insurance, and a whole host of other costs. There is also a lot of paperwork involved, and the implications of not doing these things properly can be disastrous. The IRS and other federal and state agencies, including your state's unemployment compensation insurance agency and workers' compensation insurance agency, do not look kindly upon mistakes or unfiled documentation.

It looks like a clear-cut case for hiring independent contractors, right? But unfortunately the IRS and other federal and state agencies don't much like it when businesses do that. The IRS and state tax departments dislike it because they don't receive the same level of taxes and because it can be easier to hide income as an IC. The federal and state labor agencies don't like IC arrangements because they aren't able to easily control workplace treatment and protection for ICs. Consequently these agencies place a lot of rules on the hiring of independent contractors. If you hire an IC that the IRS or another agency thinks should have been classified an employee, you can face audits, back taxes, and large fines.

The main rules of thumb for hiring an independent contractor are that she:

- owns her own business

- is generally able to choose where to do her work

- also makes her services directly available to the public

- can only be let go based on the terms of the IC agreement

- uses her own materials and supplies

- is paid a flat rate for a project, rather than by the hour

- has multiple clients

- works on a finite project rather than offer services in perpetuity

- can determine how best to go about her work, rather than heeding instructions

- is not trained by the people who hire her

- sets her own work hours

- the services she provides are not central to the day-to-day operation of the business that hired her

- has the professional skills necessary to carry out the tasks she is hired for

- does not receive workplace benefits

- pays her own taxes

You may be worrying at this point—these rules are hard to follow. Some people point to precedent, though you cannot rely in total on it. Because it is common precedent in our industry to hire independent contractors for many things, such as teaching public classes, there is a line of thought that we are all protected in doing so. That's not necessarily so. Precedent may help your case, but you should know that it does not make it a slam dunk.

There are some excellent resources at the back of this book to provide additional help in making decisions about whether to hire independent contractors or employees and, once you've chosen, to help you carry out your decision. And don't be put off. The risk that someone will challenge your hiring of ICs over employees is relatively low. The IRS or another agency might take a look at your classification of workers if, by chance, you were flagged for an IRS audit, or if someone filed a complaint against you with a state or federal agency. Still, weigh the decision carefully—a problem in this area can be financially devastating.

Bringing in a partner
Another way to grow your business is by bringing in a business partner. This can be an excellent way to get help without the issues involved with employees or independent contractors. With a partner, you can truly share the load. You get someone who is personally invested in seeing the business succeed, which means you are likely to get someone's best and most focused work. A good partner will also do whatever it takes, rather than knocking off when work hours are over. The disadvantages are that you may have to give up 100% control of your ship, and if you

are temperamentally unsuited to each other or begin to disagree on major points of direction, things can get very difficult. But with the right person, two can definitely be more than the sum of their parts, and sharing the responsibility, joys, and disappointments can be a great relief and make the work that much more fun, too.

Of course, if you decide to bring in a partner, even if you're married to them or have been best friends since diapers, put everything in writing. Even if you don't run into conflicts, having your business plan detail who is responsible for what, and having a process for how decisions are made and profits shared, all in writing, makes for a smoother sailing ship.

CASE STUDY

Patricia knew it was time to get some help. Now that her business was doing so well she just couldn't keep up with all the tasks involved in operating and marketing it while still taking good care of clients, too. She considered hiring help, but wasn't sure she wanted the responsibility of looking after an employee. She shared her ruminations with Suzie, a close friend from college, and it turned out that her friend was considering moving back to the area but hadn't found work yet. What's more, she had a degree in business and loved dogs. They decided to team up, and Suzie joined the business as a partner. Now Patricia works with clients and Suzie runs the business, and as a result, the business has taken off and Patricia enjoys being freed from the bulk of the business tasks—and the camaraderie of a shared endeavor.

Teaming up with another business

Another creative solution to grow is to team up either officially or in a loose affiliation with another business. For example, you might join forces with another dog pro based on complementary services. Perhaps you do private training and often get calls for public classes. Maybe another trainer in the area teaches classes but doesn't offer privates. You could each expand your services, or you could band together to share clients. Whether you actually legally combine the businesses or simply share some common expenses and tasks, you will both benefit. You can, for example, share marketing expenses and efforts. You could centralize scheduling and supply orders. If you find someone with complementary skills—say one of you is great at marketing and the other at organizing—you may be able to cut each person's workloads and more effectively play to each of your strengths.

CASE STUDIES

Sonja and Tammy were both excellent public class instructors. Sonja taught primarily puppy and obedience based classes, whereas Tammy focused on agility and specialized classes such as Canine Good Citizen and tricks. Old friends from training school, they often commiserated over the difficulty of finding and keeping class spaces, and the time and money spent on marketing. It finally occurred to them to team up. Combining their resources enabled them to lease a dedicated space and get more marketing value for their money and efforts. And because one's class content complemented the others so well, clients had many choices to bring them back after the first class.

Monica met Dana, another pet sitter, at a dinner party thrown by a mutual friend. They shared stories of the hassles and expense of trying to market their businesses. They also talked about difficult clients they'd had and traded their best animal war stories. At the end of the evening they agreed it had felt great to talk to someone else who understood what it was like to be an independent pet sitter. At home later that night Monica was struck with an idea. She called Dana the next day and, over coffee, they outlined a plan for a loose coalition of pet sitters that would pool resources for marketing and meet regularly for support and good company. Over time they've found that the larger scale marketing they can afford as a group has brought them all an increase in their client base, and that the monthly meetings have been a great source of ideas, support, and collegiality.

Interns and assistants

Offering unpaid internships or assistant positions can also take pressure off. People are often happy to trade their time for experience, education, or sometimes even just time with dogs. It is common for group class instructors and daycares to have assistants, for example. Some assistants help out as a hobby and a way to be around dogs, but many give their time because they want to learn dog training or the daycare ropes. Creating a strong, supportive atmosphere may lead some of these people to eventually become ICs or employees. Trainers can also use assistants or interns in their private practices, particularly when working with dog or human aggression issues. Again, the helper gains experience and knowledge from the mentoring trainer. Dog walkers and pet sitters might also consider such an approach for short term relief. The obvious advantage of this approach is free labor; the disadvantage a high turnover in most cases. Still, it can be a good stop-gap measure.

Chapter 8

FEELING THE BURN: AVOIDING PROFESSIONAL BURNOUT

No business owner completely escapes burnout—it simply comes with the territory. However, there are strategies anyone can adopt to prevent the most common headaches and keep energized. The benefits of keeping a regular schedule and having realistic expectations are obvious, though no less important for that reason, whereas other potential trouble spots, like giving free advice and being too generous with yourself on the phone, rarely occur to people until there's a real problem. Considering such potential sore spots up front, the ones that will otherwise become raw and bothered, will save you a world of frustration down the road.

How about Tuesday at 6?—What a schedule can do for you

One pitfall of self-employment is the lack of a routine. If a flexible schedule without a boss and specific deadlines makes you feel rudderless, working for yourself can be a challenge. It's easy to do little or nothing when you have unlimited time. I've seen dog pros struggle for months to do what could have been done in weeks or even days. To keep yourself working toward your goals without losing focus, make a realistic schedule and commit to deadlines. Avoid losing time by structuring your workdays carefully. What days will you see clients? When will you work on training plans? When will you take care of administrative tasks? When will you spend time growing your business?

It's easy to see how tending to your business can fall through the cracks when you add together life responsibilities such as family and the inevitable appointments with doctors and auto mechanics along with personal goals like exercise, spending time with friends and one's own dogs—not to mention just trying to enjoy some free time. A good schedule can help you manage your work and personal responsibilities as efficiently as possible, which in turn will allow you more time for personal goals. And a schedule can relieve anxiety by eliminating the need to worry about what you're forgetting or fret about things not getting done.

There are many ways to approach scheduling, and it's important to pick a style that matches your temperament. Here are two formats to consider.

The guideline schedule
A guideline schedule is a good choice if you're looking for plenty of flexibility and enjoy a high degree of self discipline. In this schedule you assign days or blocks of time to various possible tasks. For example, you might relegate weekday afternoons to paperwork, down time, or errands. You then can decide each week or each day how to spend your time, based on your own desires and what needs to be done.

The detailed schedule
If you have a procrastinator's tendencies, often feel disorganized, and know that you need structure to thrive, the detailed schedule can help you run your business smoothly. This schedule assigns days and blocks of time to each task and is followed in the same format each week. It provides a rhythm and order that ensures a place for everything, and removes the daily worry over how best to spend time, and the guilt over not spending it the way you think you should. With this schedule, work time is clearly defined, and when it's time for play you need not feel guilty.

Lumping vs. splitting
Dog trainers, thanks to Bob Bailey, often talk about lumping vs. splitting when making criteria decisions. I like to apply this concept to scheduling. It's a work style choice: do you prefer to focus on one thing for an extended period of time, or do you feel more comfortable frequently shifting tasks? Would you rather do your business paperwork in one fell swoop? Then assign it to one day a week and clear as much else away from that day as possible. For example, a trainer might get up and walk the dog or exercise in the morning, lump administrative work from 11-4, then prep for evening clients and have dinner before leaving for the evening training sessions.

Generally speaking, it is more efficient to work this way, as you lose time with each transition from one task to another. But if focusing on one thing for long periods of time is not your work style, or the nature of your business doesn't allow for it, or you have unsavory tasks you can't face in large doses, you can split things into smaller portions. A dog walker who is home from walking late each afternoon could assign herself administrative work in two smaller sessions on Tuesday and Thursday after walking.

General scheduling tips

Start with a fresh piece of paper and mark off the days of the week, without any actual dates (or use a computer calendar program). If working on paper use a pencil. You can also have several sheets in order to try multiple approaches and be able to compare them side by side.

On another sheet make a list of all your tasks and obligations, and all the other things you want time for. Organize the list into categories—one for your business, one for any other work obligations you might have, and one for your personal and home life. You can break the categories down into smaller pieces if that's helpful to you.

Plug in tasks or commitments with set times first. For example, if you go to yoga classes twice a week, put them down—they're the same time every week and you can't change them.

Next consider any items that have general time constraints. For example, if you will be teaching classes, you know that they're generally taught M-Th evenings and Sat/Sun daytimes. Dogs have to be walked M-F daytimes.

Look at the remaining items and the openings on your schedule. Think about your own work patterns and daily rhythms. For example, are you most alert and focused in the morning? Perhaps one or more morning slots would be best for business paperwork. Do you find yourself a little sleepy in the afternoon? This would be a good time to schedule in the daily walk with your own dogs.

Don't forget other peoples' schedules, too. If seeing friends more often is a priority, be sure to consider their work schedules.

Setting boundaries around the phone

The phone is a tough issue for small dog service businesses. We all know the scenario—you return a message that is an hour old and hear, "Oh, thanks, but I've already found someone." One or two of these experiences is all it takes for many dog pro business owners to frantically reach for the phone at the first ring, at any hour of day or night, weekday or weekend. And, of course, to carry that cell phone everywhere, rushing out of restaurants and movies when it vibrates.

It's a quandary. If you let the phone rule you, you become tired and burned-out from constantly being on call. You also teach your clients to expect your availability at all times, thus perpetuating the evil circle. On the other hand, no one wants to lose the potential clients. What to do?

I strongly urge having off hours—hours that your business is closed and the ringer is turned off. You might lose a few clients, but you are likely to enjoy your work much more and stay in the business for the long haul. A few clients now are not worth an early career change.

There are also ways to lessen the negative effect of turning the ringer off. When you choose your set phone hours, for example, try to include the most common times the phone rings so that you catch the majority of calls. Spend some time on your outgoing message—what people hear when you don't pick up can make a difference. Perhaps you're out training or walking or caring for an animal—make sure to sound interesting and professional. Also include the hours you are available by phone and/or when to expect a return call, and consider mentioning your website, in case people want to get more detailed information about your business.

Think about getting help with the phone. Though you are probably the best at selling what you have to offer, the right person can be effective for you, and it's better than a message machine. When you're first starting out perhaps a friend or family member would be willing to pilot the phone for a couple hours a day. Once you're established and growing well you may choose to pay someone for this service, or to pay someone for other work so that you are free to answer the phone and sell your service.

Set clear expectations—for clients and of them
First of all, go back and re-read the rates section in Chapter 6. Remind yourself that you are worth what you charge and that you needn't apologize for being paid for your professional knowledge and skill.

See your clients as you see their dogs
One of the things I love about positive reinforcement dog training is the perspective it gives us on problems. When a dog does something we don't like we calmly say to ourselves, "The dog is doing X. I would like him to do Y. How will I help him to make that change?" It's so understanding, so humane, so respectful—and so effective. We don't waste time and energy fuming over his naughtiness. We don't judge him to be bad because he's engaging in undesirable behavior. We assume he can do better, and we see our task as one of enacting and supporting change.

I urge you to view your human clients this way, too. Many dog pros I worked with when I was Director of Behavior and Training at the San Francisco SPCA spent a lot of energy on their feelings about their clients. It's easy to be judgmental of peoples' attitudes toward their dogs, or their treatment of them. It's easy to be frustrated by their lack of skill or progress. But spending too much time on these emotions generally means missing solutions. When we decide a dog is a bad dog, we limit our options for treatment. Such a judgment of temperament often leads to a battle of wills. This is so much less useful than "The dog is doing X. I would like him to do Y. How will I help him to make that change?" It's similar with humans. When we decide a client is bad or stubborn or stupid, it leaves us with few options. How different if, instead, we see their potential. My client is now doing X when her dog does not sit. I would like her to do Y. How will I help her to make this change? Or, my client now believes X about dog behavior. I want her to understand Y. How will I help her to make this change? Now you're cooking—you have a clearly stated question for which to generate an answer. You can formulate a game plan instead of throwing up your hands in despair. As an industry we've learned to show dogs compassion and patience while we work to change their behavior. Our behavior modification plans demonstrate a step by step approach and the understanding that solid changes in behavior can take time. Try approaching the human component of training the same way—it will temper your expectations, keeping frustration at bay.

People can learn new ideas and acquire new skills. Be patient, and remember to notice your clients' little changes, their bits of progress, and reinforce those—just as you would with a dog.

CASE STUDY

Stuart despaired after his first solo public class session with dogs. He lamented, "I just don't understand it! I told them at orientation—I explained all about punishment, and all about Gentle Leaders and everything, but two people—they still brought their dogs in on choke chains!" After he calmed down we talked for a while about his goals for his students and about the various reasons why they might be using choke chains. Then we laid out a game plan for gently moving the clients towards equipment alternatives and a new way of thinking about training. Stuart reported back to me at the end of the class. Beaming, he said, "One is using a GL and the other is using an Easy Walk harness! And last night at graduation I heard one of the parents telling all the other students about how great the GL is and recommending it to them! I think they're both going to sign up for the next class!"

Be the expert, be the professional, take charge

Remember that you are the expert, and let that govern your behavior with clients. I don't mean to suggest being pushy, bossy, condescending, or arrogant. I mean for you to be professional. For example, when you are doing a phone interview avoid behaving as though you're on a job interview. You are the professional. Take control of the interview—be the interviewer instead of the interviewee. You aren't begging for a job; you're screening a potential client. And when you go to a client's home, set the tone from the beginning. For example, after the initial hellos, gently but firmly take charge: "Shall we sit at the kitchen table?" Then set the expectations. Trainers might say something like, "As I described on the phone, I'd like to take some time to get more detailed information on what's going on with Pongo. Then we can discuss options for meeting your goals." Walkers, you might begin with, "The purpose of my interview is to learn more about Otis so that I can be sure to place him with other dogs whose company he will enjoy." By setting the tone from the beginning you will be more easily able to direct the conversation and gather the information you need. Your confidence also helps clients build their confidence in you, which is particularly helpful when you suggest further services or are introducing them to a philosophy of training or care which is new to them.

CASE STUDY

Janet was furious. She had had her third session with Rich and his dog Hooch, and Rich's treatment of her had been rude, disrespectful, and dismissive. "I start to tell him about the next exercise when he interrupts me and says, 'Naw, I don't want to do that. Let's do something else.' And he keeps calling me 'Girl' and telling me that this 'treat slinging' isn't real training. He doesn't do any homework, but keeps letting me come back. It's infuriating." After some reflection on the situation and its causes, we made a game plan. Janet strode into the next appointment with confident posture and said firmly, before Rich had a chance to speak, "You are paying me for professional training services, for which I am certified and highly qualified. You have said you would like your dog to listen to you and be more focused. I can help you make that happen, but you will have to follow my instructions. If you find you cannot or will not, then you will need to find another trainer, as I have many clients who would like the benefit of my services." Without a hint of a pause, she continued, "Now, today we will work on three exercises. The first one looks like this…" She later laughed about the change in Rich. "He still tests me a bit from time to time, but overall he follows my lead, and he and Hooch are making a lot of progress. The best part is when I hear him tell his wife the things I've told him. Of course, he makes it sound like the ideas are all his, but that's okay with me!"

Performance expectations—homework, progress, etc.

In the world of dog training one size rarely fits all. The ideal behavior modification or training plan from a professional perspective may not work in a home environment, particularly if we are talking about a typical American household with busy schedules and a day-to-day life of barely contained chaos. We often discuss how to set dogs up for success—well, why not do the same for our human clients?

Wherever possible, design training plans with your clients' strengths and lifestyles in mind. The idea of "Nothing For Free" is a great example of this—the idea of asking a dog to practice behaviors in exchange for all the small daily rewards of life—going through doors, being fed, being petted, having a ball thrown, etc. Many owners are more likely to learn this way of interacting with their dogs more easily than changing their patterns to incorporate formal training sessions. Plus the dog learns obedience in daily situations, rather than with the attendant environmental cues of a training session. Designing plans that fit individual lifestyles takes extra creativity, but will greatly increase compliance.

Also attempt to give clients choices wherever possible. These might come in the form of service choices (such as in home training versus day training versus board and train—see Chapter 6). Other choices might include the order of goals to address, how to structure training sessions, or a choice between exercises. Of course, some situations lend themselves to the giving of choices while others require a more set regimen.

Firing clients

If you want to enjoy your business for many years to come, I recommend not forcing yourself to work with dogs or humans that cause you undue stress. There is no failure involved in firing a dog or human client. It's unreasonable to think that every match will be perfect. If you have a dog that is not working out, whether because you don't feel safe, or feel that your skills aren't the right match, or even because you simply do not enjoy the dog's company, you do no kindness to yourself, the client, or the dog by continuing. And if a human client causes unwarranted worry or difficulty, whether due to lack of compliance or poor attitude or a personality clash, your business is better off in the long run if you sever the relationship.

Sometimes it makes sense to be straightforward with a client about why you are ending services. If you feel you are not the right match or that the dog is unhappy or unsafe, just say so. For example, perhaps an asocial dog is miserable in a pack walking or daycare setting. You've tried to incorporate her and make her comfortable, but you are not seeing progress. You might suggest private walks instead. If you feel a training case is not making progress, suggest another trainer who might have more experience with that type of issue.

When you are letting a client go for reasons that have more to do with the dog or owner, you have to decide how honest to be. If the dog is dangerous, it's your professional responsibility to say so, and to document this in writing for your own liability protection. When a human client has been difficult, being upfront is a bit harder. If it's an issue of compliance, I would advise being honest, but if you're dealing with a temperament or personality issue, you may not feel comfortable saying so—and often that approach is not constructive anyway. To avoid unnecessary conflict you can use a general deflection—that you don't feel the progress being made is satisfactory, or that the group you're walking is not a good match for the dog, or that your schedule has changed such that you cannot accommodate daily visits to their home, etc.

"Oh! You're a dog trainer! My dog does this thing…" Avoid giving away free advice.

We've all been there—at a party, or in line at the grocery store, or at a child's soccer game. Wherever it happens, you know how it goes. Someone asks you what you do. You tell them. Next thing you know you're listening to their dog problems and being pumped for free advice. And it's a funny thing—we often feel compelled to give it. Sometimes because we don't know how to get out of doing so, sometimes because we love what we do and enjoy talking about it, and often because we care about dogs and want to see them get the help they need.

But it's a losing proposition for all involved to give free advice. It cheats you out of business and devalues your professional knowledge and skill, it reduces the chance the dog owner will pursue the help he or she needs, and it doesn't get the dog any real help. Advice given in a social situation is seldom followed—and you can't offer the kind of detail and support that most cases require.

Setting boundaries for public and social spaces

Few people are aware of the level of education and experience a qualified trainer possesses, of the amount of information needed to diagnose a behavior, and of the degree of thought put into a behavior modification plan. As a result, they don't feel shy about asking for quick-fix tips. The trick to handling these situations is to politely avoid giving too much free advice while creating the highest likelihood that they will actually seek your professional help. Here is a strategy you can try:

1. Interrupt

2. Empathize

3. Build Confidence

4. Redirect

5. Tip (optional)

6. End

Interrupt. Let's say a woman begins her story, "My little dog Rin Tin Tin barks so loudly you'd think she was a German Shepherd, or even two dogs! Drives me crazy. She barks all day long. One time she even…"

This is a good time for step 1, the interruption. Allow the other person to tell just enough of the story to give you a hint of the problem, but don't let them get going full swing. The more they invest in the story, the harder it will be for you to avoid their request for immediate answers and explanations. Intervene in a friendly and assertive manner, and try to be reinforcing to soften the interruption. "Sounds like Rin Tin Tin is quite the character! Amazing how little dogs can have such big personalities."

Empathize. Immediately make it clear that you've heard their concern: "Barking, especially when it's constant, can be so frustrating! It's hard to hear yourself think!"

Build confidence. This is the time to elegantly let them know you're an expert and that diagnosis and treatment is taken seriously in the world of professional dog training. "That kind of barking can be many things—demand barking, barrier frustration, alarm barking, separation anxiety…"

Redirect. This is your opportunity to suggest your services, which also gently but clearly implies that you require payment for your expertise.

"To know for sure what makes Rin Tin Tin bark, I would need to do a complete diagnostic interview. Then I can work with you to design a treatment plan to best suit your needs. Here's my card if you'd like to do that. You can also take a look at my website to learn a little more about what I do and to see my background and credentials. I'd be delighted to work with you and Rin Tin Tin to see if we can't create a nice, quiet house for you."

If you're really gung-ho and have a feeling they wouldn't mind, you might ask for their contact information (but don't scribble on the backs of receipts, carry around a small book for this) so you can follow up with them.

Tip (Optional). If you think it's warranted, tip them by offering a management or training suggestion. An example for Rin Tin Tin's mom might be, "In the meantime, here's one thing you can do that might help: Reward him any time he's not barking. If you notice the house is quiet, take a moment to give him a cookie or a belly rub. Let him know that you appreciate the peace." Depending on the situation, your aim could be to offer a measure with immediate effect in order to build confidence in your ability to help. Other times you might present a management suggestion to diminish risk or to create some improvement in the life of either the owner or the dog.

End. It's important now to end the conversation. If you don't, it's likely the person will jump in to ask follow-up questions or tell you additional information or stories about their dog, which puts you right back in the hot seat. If you're in a situation where you can walk away, do so. "It was really nice meeting you and hearing about Rin Tin Tin. I hope you'll let me know if I can be of help. Have a great day now!" If you're trapped—in a line or waiting room, for example, change the subject. "By the way, do you happen to know what the weather is supposed to be like this weekend? I've been hearing all sorts of conflicting reports. I'm putting on a birthday party this weekend and not sure whether to plan it for inside or out in the garden. It's for my little niece. If she had it her way, we'd..."

Additional advice on giving advice
Though the six steps are broken down for you here, in practice they run together and overlap. Try not to pause, as a determined dog storyteller always will look for a way back in. And practice makes perfect—though it may seem a little silly, try practicing this technique in the shower or while you're driving. Recall a past situation where you were ambushed with "A dog trainer! My dog..." story. Re-enact the scene in your head with these

six steps. The more you train yourself to respond this way, the easier it'll be next time you find yourself cornered at a dinner party.

Finally, be aware of the ethical and liability issues that sometimes lurk in these conversations. For example, if the situation described to you is potentially dangerous for the dog or other people, or if it sounds like the dog's quality of life is threatened, you may feel compelled to have a longer discussion. But be careful—advice given in public or social contexts can never be as complete as you would want it to be, and you do not have a contract to help cover your liability. Center your advice in Step 5 (Tipping) around management suggestions to reduce any potential risk to the dog or humans. You may want to use Steps 2, 3, and 4 (Empathizing, Building Confidence, and Redirecting) to attempt to impress the seriousness of the situation upon them. Be firm but gentle, as some people may not be ready to hear the bad news. If they feel overwhelmed or perceive an attack they will be less likely to call you or another trainer for help. Ask for contact information so you can follow up and schedule a proper consultation.

Walkers, sitters, and daycare operators—be particularly careful in giving training advice in social or professional situations. Without certification you may be at a higher level of liability risk if you give advice that spills over into areas of training. It's safer and more appropriate to refer clients to a dog trainer for training questions.

Setting boundaries for friends and family

The above strategy becomes a lot harder to use when friends and family are involved. But it's very important to have boundaries here, too—especially if you have a lot of friends and family members who have dogs! Dealing with the problem dogs of loved ones can be a serious source of burnout for several reasons; for one thing, friends and family often have the worst compliance, perhaps because there's no sense of urgency—you'll always be there. Also, research shows that people in our culture simply don't value what they don't pay for, including advice. And that double whammy—lack of compliance and lack of professional regard—can cause tension. It's frustrating to see your advice ignored, and I've seen cases where family or friends blame the trainer when the problem isn't solved, even when the cause of failure is a clear lack of compliance. You can imagine the painful dynamics there. In summary, if you have heard the sayings about not working with family or living with friends, add to that not training friends' and family members' dogs.

But how do you avoid it? Gingerly would be an understatement. Try to think (and I urge you to do this proactively if it's not too late) of an explanation that would make sense to that person, and come across supportive and caring and not as a brush off. Some I have suggested to others in that situation have included:

"I feel I'm too close to you and Tramp to get a good perspective on this (or to be effective)… Let me find another trainer to bring in for a fresh set of eyes."

"This is a little out of my area of knowledge or expertise. I know this awesome trainer who would be able to help. Let me go grab her number."

"I won't be able to give you the help you need over the phone—this is something that really needs doing in person. Let me find a good trainer in your area."

If these don't feel like they'd work for you, think about the specifics of your case and look for the out. And of course if you can just talk straight—"I have this policy, and here's why…" that's great.

Certainly there will be cases you feel comfortable taking or are compelled to accept. I hope you'll keep them to an absolute minimum, but if you do find yourself in that situation, follow your best practices. Set a professional tone at the beginning of each session and do not allow yourself to be pulled off topic. And try not to talk about the training much in between sessions. If you see your dad or sister at the dinner table and they start asking follow up questions, cut it off with some version of "Hmm… interesting. Let me think about that when I have my trainer brain on and I'll come up with something for our next session."

CASE STUDY

I was talking about burnout to a group of dog trainers preparing to graduate from an advanced training program, and Amanda nodded her head gravely when I spoke about the dangers of working with friends and family. "You have a story, I take it?" She laughed. "Boy, do I! When I was a newlywed I agreed to do some training for my husband's parents. Their little dog was still urinating in the house on a frequent basis—and was 4 years old. So I went over the whole housetraining protocol for them, even lent them a crate and got the dog used to it. They quickly undid her comfort with the crate by using it as a punishment—even though I warned against that—and, 3 years later, she's still peeing in the house. Which means that at every family function I get a full report on my failure as a trainer: 'Well, Petunia peed in Harvey's den again this morning, and she still won't go near that box you brought over!' Drives me crazy! At first, I would try to re-explain, to remind them the steps, but my mother in law would just say, 'No, we already tried that—you said that last time.' I tell you, avoid working for friends or family if you possibly can!"

Pro bono work

I generally discourage pro bono work. Many of my clients want to help people who cannot afford professional services, and I commend that. But as a way of serving this goal, pro bono work—offering your services to individuals for free—has many unintended consequences.

One concern is compliance burnout. We often do not value what we don't pay for, and many trainers finds that pro bono clients have a low rate of compliance. Now there are exceptions to this, too. A lot depends on how you screen your clients. Pro bono clients who are truly in financial need but very committed to their animals can be the best clients you'll ever have. I have also seen many trainers talked down in their prices or into fully pro bono work by people who perhaps did not truly meet the standards of financial hardship but instead were clever bargain hunters, and the results were frustrating.

But it is always a dilemma. How can you really screen individuals without asking for financial records? It's tough, and there are many legal implications in setting up such a system.

The other potential hazard with pro bono work is getting a reputation for it. If you are trying to run a business for income you do not want to become known as the go-to person for pro bono work. Your phone will soon be ringing off the hook as every trainer in your area sends people your way who have balked at their prices or shared a sob story.

If you want to dedicate a portion of your time to less privileged dog owners consider volunteering your time rather than offering pro bono services. Volunteer to answer a hotline at the local shelter, or to make yourself available there for public training on certain days for a set number of hours. This way the shelter can do the screening and you can offer your services without tripping up your own business.

If you do choose to engage in pro bono work, set clear boundaries. For example, give yourself a rule of no more than X number of pro bono cases at any given time.

You Can't Be Everything To Yourself—Contract It Out!

When you run a small business you have to oversee everything. You may be an excellent dog walker but are you ready to be a bookkeeper, accountant, marketing manager, secretary, and office manager? A key to successful full-time business ownership is to recognize your weaknesses and subcontract tasks that confound you or that require expertise you don't possess.

List the skills required to run your business. Then ask yourself: what are you good at? Where do your interests lie? Which tasks can you readily do? Which will stress you, weaken the business, or possibly be left undone? For those, get help. Trade skills with a friend or hire a contractor or professional service provider.

Chapter 9

PARTING SHOTS: A FEW EXTRA PIECES OF ADVICE

For most people starting a business is fraught with anxiety. You work so hard and can't help but have expectations and hopes for things to come along quickly—particularly clients and revenue!—and despair sets in fast when they don't. I've seen people give up on their businesses far too soon because the pressure got to them—but there is no reason to let that happen to you.

The six month rule

First, set reasonable expectations. Anticipate that any marketing effort you make will take a minimum of six months to yield strong results, and if that seems like a long time to you, it might help to envision how marketing works. Say a potential client picks up your brochure with the intention of calling, but happens to place it beneath the take-out menus, only to uncover it months later and think, "You know, I should really do that!" Or someone takes home a class schedule but finds she's just too busy to fit anything new in—until her dog steals the Thanksgiving turkey and she decides she's had enough and where did she put that flyer? Another person might have read your first two newsletters at his vet's office, but it was the article on resource guarding in the third one that prompted him to call. Just because the phone doesn't ring as soon as you make your efforts doesn't mean it won't. Give people time to think about things and to be ready.

Ride the waves

But you don't have to just sit and wait, either—nor should you. Remember from Chapter 4 that you should be spending at least 30% of your time on marketing, especially in the beginning. I recommend marketing in waves. Implement a marketing project and then, while you're waiting to see how it goes, start the next project on your list. Once that's underway, begin marketing project number three.

Marketing in waves has two advantages for you. First, it keeps you busy while you wait. There is no better antidote to the stresses of waiting than productive activity. Second, it helps your business grow faster and more consistently as each marketing wave, or project, hits the shore, bringing additional clients. Consistent marketing helps smooth out some of the client dry spells that often plague dog pros. You're also hedging your bets—if one project's results are disappointing, another is right on its heels to help.

Trainer error or, "it's not working!"

When something isn't working, positive reinforcement trainers know to look at themselves before blaming the dog or owner. Was there trainer error? Before you decide your business is impossible, check for a dog pro error before giving up. Are you truly putting in the marketing effort and time? Are your efforts in line with the marketing maxims laid out in Chapter 4? Have you set at least three waves in motion and waited six months to a year for the effect?

Eventually you can go into a maintenance mode with your marketing, simply renewing the initiatives that have proved the most fruitful. But in the beginning, or anytime you look for active growth, keep busy and be patient.

Click yourself—keeping perspective

I've found that many of my clients over the years are quick to disparage themselves and focus on the negative in the first couple years of owning a business. When you're having a rough day, or week, try giving yourself a little R+—remember, positive reinforcement is powerful stuff! Literally sit down with paper and pen and list the things you've gotten done, milestones you've hit, efforts you've made, things you've learned, clients you've helped. Note how far you have come. Sometimes when things don't happen at the speed we wish for it feels like nothing is happening at all. But you may be surprised by the progress you are making if you stop to click yourself for it.

Resources

1. Business Resources

Insurance Agents
Leslie Dodds (CA only)
leslie-dodds@leavitt.com
707 284 5912

Dennis Stowers
dstowers@mourerfoster.com
800 686 2663 ext. 230

Legal Assistance

Service Mark and Name Issues
Kelly McCarthy, service mark attorney & dog trainer
kmccarthy@sideman.com
415 733 3923

Trademarks: Legal Care For Your Business and Product Name
www.nolopress.com

Employee and Independent Contractor Issues
How to Safely and Legally Hire Independent Contractors
www.nolopress.com (includes all forms you need!)

Hiring Independent Contractors
www.nolopress.com

The Employer's Legal Handbook
www.nolopress.com

Contracts
dogTEC dogPRO cd
www.dogtec.org

Bookkeepers and Accountants

American Institute of Professional Bookkeepers
www.aipb.org

Book Keeper List
www.bookkeeperlist.com
"A resource center for bookkeepers and for those looking for one."

Book Keeping Help
www.bookkeepinghelp.com
US and Canadian directory for bookkeepers, accountants, and tax preparers

Market Research
www.demographicsguru.com

www.demographicsnow.com

Your local Chamber of Commerce

Marketing Materials and Designers
Bangarang Media
www.bangarangmedia.com
dan@phairas.com
logo development, print materials, web design, writing for websites and print materials

Sniff Design
www.sniffdesign.com
monica@sniffdesign.com
logo development, print materials, and web design

JT Dataworks
www.jtdataworks.com
judy@jtdataworks.com
web design and web optimization specialist

Dogs of Hudson
www.dogsofhudson.com
erica@dogsofhudson.com
writing for websites and print marterials

MPhotography
www.mphotography.com
jenniferdmurray@yahoo.com
stock dog photography and photo shoots in the SF Bay Area

Candid Canines Photography
www.candidcanines.com
stock dog photography

dogTEC Business Support Services
www.dogtec.org
info@dogtec.org
veronica@dogtec.org

- Business support coaching, case consults, curriculum consults.

- Support products, including the dogPRO CDs for trainers and walkers and sitters, behavior modification plans cd.

- Client homework CD available 2008.

- dogPRO curriculum packages and DVDs available 2008, 2009

- Free email business newsletter—email info@dogtec.org for a free subscription

2. Education Resources

For Trainers

Training Schools

San Francisco SPCA Academy for Dog Trainers with Jean Donaldson
San Francisco, CA
www.sfspca.org/academy

Marin Humane Society Canine Behavior Academy with Trish King
Novato, CA
www.marinhumanesociety.org/

Peaceable Paws with Pat Miller
www.peaceablepaws.com
Hagerstown, MD

Coaching People To Train Their Dogs Course with Terry Ryan
www.legacycanine.com
Sequim, WA

Karen Pryor Academy and Dog Trainer Certification
www.clickertraining.com

Raising Canine Beginning Dog Trainer's Course
www.raisingcanine.com
Online course

Animal Behavior College
www.animalbehaviorcollege.com
Online course augmented with local mentorships

American College of Applied Science
www.animalbehaviorcounselors.org
MS degree in Companion Animal Behavior Counseling

Companion Animal Sciences Institute
www.casinstitute.com

Continuing Education Seminars

Association of Pet Dog Trainers
www.apdt.com

Dogs of Course
www.dogsofcourse.com

dogTEC
www.dogTEC.org

International Association of Advanced Behavior Consultants
www.iaabc.org

Monadnock Canine Academy
www.monadpets.org

Positively Trained
www.positivelytrained.com

Puppyworks
www.puppyworks.com

Raising Canine (telecourses)
www.raisingcanine.com

San Francisco SPCA
www.sfspca.org/academy

Websites, Blogs, and Online Discussion Groups

www.apdt.com

clickersolutions@yahoo.com

peaceablepaws@yahoo.com

www.dogstardaily.com

Recommended Books
This is by no means a comprehensive list and you shouldn't stop here!

Culture Clash, Jean Donaldson

How To Teach an Old Dog New Tricks, Ian Dunbar

Don't Shoot The Dog, Karen Pryor

Exel-erated Learning, Pam Reid

Canine Body Language: A Photographic Guide, Brenda Aloff

The Domestic Dog, James Serpell

Aggressive Behavior in Dogs: A Comprehensive Technical Manual for Professionals, James O'Heare

Dog Language: An Encyclopedia of Canine Behavior, 2nd Edition, Roger Abrantes

Dogs Behaving Badly, Nicholas Dodman

Coaching People To Train Their Dogs, Terry Ryan

Dogs Bite But Balloons and Bedroom Slippers Are More Dangerous, Janis Bradley

Book and DVD Sources

Dogwise
www.dogwise.com

Tawzer Video
www.tawzerdogvideos.com

Associations, Accreditation

Association of Pet Dog Trainers
www.apdt.com

International Association of Advanced Behavior Counselors
www.iabbc.org

For Dog Walkers and Daycares
I've placed dog walkers and daycares together because their educational needs are so similar—a real emphasis on dog-dog behavior, pack composition and management, and reading body language.

Schools and Accreditation
dogTEC Dog Walking Academy
www.dogTEC.org

dogTEC Dog Walking Academy Telecourse
www.dogTEC.org

Continuing Education Seminars, Books, & DVDs

I recommend attending dog training seminars, and purchasing dog training books and DVDs, particularly those with an emphasis on body language and dog-dog related issues. See sources above.

For Pet Sitters

Education Seminars

National Association of Professional Pet Sitters Annual Conference
www.napps.org

Pet Sitters International Quest Conference
www.psi.org

Basic dog training education will be helpful, too—see resources above.

Books

Pet Sitting for Profit, Patti Moran

Online Discussion Groups

google.com/Top/Recreation/Pets/Sitters_and_Walkers/

Associations and Accreditation

National Association of Professional Pet Sitters (NAPPS)
www.petsitters.org
Membership includes a quarterly newsletter.

Pet Sitters International (PSI)
www.petsit.com
Membership includes The World of Professional Pet Sitting magazine.

3. Budget Considerations

A word on business plans and budgets:

Unless you are seeking funding, you will not need a formal business plan. Following the advice in each chapter of this book will reward you with an informal business plan to guide you as you move forward to start or grow your enterprise. Should you require a formal plan, you'll soon realize that there are more templates to choose from than you could possibly need. It's best to ask the funding sources you will be petitioning what they want to see in a solid plan. If they have a specific template, all the better. In the absence of such direction, Palo Alto Software has a good product with several dog-related samples. www.paloalto.com

Here I have provided a basic list of potential start up and ongoing costs you should be aware of when doing your feasibility math.

Start Up Costs

Vehicle (if needed)

Facility (if using)

- initial lease money down or downpayment for purchase

- build out costs

Communication

- phone installation and/or cell phone purchase

- initial internet fees—service installation

Initial Marketing

- website development

- URL purchase

- design and printing

- advertising, if applicable

- other one time initial project costs specific to your plans

Professional Fees and Assistance

- paperwork fees

- contracts

- accountancy support

- lawyer, if using one

Education

- school and seminar fees

- books and DVDs

- business coaching support

Office Supplies

- hardware—computer, printer, etc.

- software—Quickbooks Pro, kennel software if needed, etc.

Dog Supplies

- trainers—training tools

- walkers—leashes, tags, first aid kit, etc.

- sitters—toys if using

- daycares—beds, dishes, toys, training aids, first aid kit, etc.

Ongoing Costs

Vehicle

- maintenance

- gas

Facility, if using

- lease or mortgage

- utilities

- phone

- repair and maintenance

- insurance

Communication

- cell phone

- internet service

Marketing

- website maintenance, hosting fees, URL renewal

- ongoing project costs

- replacement printing

- advertising, if applicable

Professional Fees and Assistance

- professional insurance

- accountancy and/or bookkeeping

Professional Development and Continuing Education

- association fees

- seminars (don't forget travel expenses for conferences)

- books and DVDs

- business support services

Office Supplies

Dog Supplies

- trainers—treats, tools, etc.

- walkers—treats, replacement leashes, etc.

- sitters—treats and toys if using

- daycares—treats, food (if supplying), replacement beds, toys, etc.

Employment or Independent Contractor Costs, if using

- pay

- payroll taxes and fees

4. Annotated Start Up To Do List

Legalities and Liabilities

	To Do	Notes	Source	X
1.	Check name availability	Be sure the name you want to use is free for use. Do a search on the national trademark sight, the state trademark and LLC/corporation site, the county site, and check to see what domain names are available (.com, etc).	www.uspto.gov your secretary of state site your county clerk site www.godaddy.com or equivalent	
2.	File for LLC Status (optional)	This is an optional step you may choose to take to increase your liability protection. You can convert to an LLC at any time. If you file as an LLC be sure to use the full business name as the "applicant" on all other steps below.	Download forms from your secretary of state site For help: www.dogtec.org www.nolopress.com Local Lawyers	
3.	Business License	Remember to proactively file a home based business exemption if needed.	Download forms from your city website, call, or walk in.	

	To Do	Notes	Source	X
4.	Fictitious Business Name	Read instructions carefully—multiple copies are often required. You will probably need to run an announcement in a local paper. If neither the FBN nor the business license need the other one completed first, go ahead and file both at the same time.	Download forms from your city website, call, or walk in.	
5.	Get Your EIN	If you've filed as an LLC or if you plan to have employees you need an EIN. Otherwise it is not required. If you apply online the form number is SS-4	Apply online at: www.irs.gov Or get your EIN over the phone by calling 1 800 829 4933	
6.	Open Business Bank Account	This is highly recommended for all businesses and required for LLCs Call your bank ahead to schedule an appointment. Be sure to ask them what paperwork to bring along.	Local bank of choice	
7.	Join a Professional Association	This is great for continuing education opportunities and it helps to professionalize your business as well as push the industry forward. Membership also provides access to professional insurance.	www.apdt.com www.iaabc.com www.napps.com www.psi.com	

	To Do	Notes	Source	X
8.	Obtain Insurance	If you're going to see clients prior to this step, get insurance first. You can always change the name on your policy if you need to.	Agents: Leslie Dodds (CA only) leslie-dodds@leavitt.com Dennis Stowers dstowers@mourer-foster.com	
9.	Purchase Contracts	Have contracts in hand before you see clients. If you will be seeing clients before this step, move this step up!	www.dogtec.org	
10.	Service Mark your Business Name (optional)	You can service mark at the state or national level. Both are optional. If you choose to pursue a national service mark you may want to engage legal assistance.	State: download forms from your secretary of state site National: www.uspto.gov Kelly McCarthy— service mark attorney and dog trainer kmccarthy@sideman.com, 415 733 3923	
11.	Learn LLC Rules & Requirements	Learn what you need to know to keep your LLC protection intact.	www.dogTEC.org www.NoloPress.com	

Marketing

While waiting for various paperwork to come back from the offices you've sent it out to, you can get to work on your marketing. See the Chapter 4 for more detailed instructions.

	To Do	Notes	Source	X
1.	Define Your Services	Decide exactly what you're going to offer, down to the details. Consider a specialized niche. Be clear about who your target clients are.	www.dogtec.org	
2.	Develop Your Marketing Message	How will you describe what you do to those you want to use your services? What makes you different? What benefits do clients stand to gain?	www.dogtec.org	
3.	Develop Your Marketing Projects	These are the vehicles that will get your message out to your audience. Choose several projects and pick one or two to implement first.	www.dogtec.org	
4.	Develop Marketing Materials	Now that you know what your projects are, you know what materials you need. Engage a designer for a professionally branded look.	See list of designers.	

Rates, Policies, and Systems

See the Chapter 6 for detailed instructions.

	To Do	Notes	Source	X
1.	Compare Local Rates	Call other local service providers (or ask a friend to call for you) to find out what they charge. Be sure to get details about their services—how much time they offer, number of sessions or walks, any extra materials, etc.		
2.	Set Your Rates	Keep all variables in mind; local rates, how your services are different or unique, what you need and want to be paid. You do not have to "apologize" for being new through your rates!	www.dogtec.org	
3.	Write Your Policies	Put together policies for payment, cancellation, geographical boundaries, and any packages you are offering. Write your policies for the future! You may not be busy now, but you will be. Make sure your policies will fit the needs of a growing business.		
4.	Design Systems and Develop or Purchase Materials for Them	You need systems and materials for phone screening, your initial intake or interview process, payment and general bookkeeping, ongoing record keeping, dog groupings and routes if applicable, client homework if applicable, etc.	www.dogtec.org Quickbooks pro software	

Scheduling

	To Do	Notes	X
1.	List All Business Duties	This includes client and dog care time as well as marketing and admin work.	
2.	List Everything Else	Include any other responsibilities, including any part or full time work, family duties, and recreational activities you wish to prioritize.	
3.	Devise a Schedule	Work to accommodate your business and personal needs as efficiently as possible.	
4.	Try It Out	Give the schedule a go and make adjustments as needed.	

5. Service Comparison Chart

Service	Best Suited For:	Best suited for clients who:	Relative client cost	Best suited for dog pros who:	Relative start up costs	Relative ongoing costs:	Relative revenue potential *	Impact on time	Other Notes
In Home Training	obedience manners puppy raising home-based issues such as digging, separation anxiety, baby prep, house training, etc.	have time and a desire to be hands on have higher end skills	expensive	have strong coaching and interpersonal skills enjoy working with people	very low	very low	moderate	work is mostly nights and weekends	can be slower training process if seen all the way through, training is likely to last can be difficult to see the process all the way through

Service	Best Suited For:	Best suited for clients who:	Relative client cost	Best suited for dog pros who:	Relative start up costs	Relative ongoing costs:	Relative revenue potential *	Impact on time	Other Notes
Day Training	obedience long-winded, technical problems such as fear and aggression	have less time and more money want their dogs to remain at home	more expensive	enjoy flexible scheduling	very low	very low	moderate	work is done during daytime, when other training work is slow	can often see faster training results faster progress often means higher client compliance

Service	Best Suited For:	Best suited for clients who:	Relative client cost	Best suited for dog pros who:	Relative start up costs	Relative ongoing costs:	Relative revenue potential *	Impact on time	Other Notes
Board & Train	obedience manners aggression	have less time and more money want immediate results	more expensive	enjoy more hands on time with dogs actively enjoy company of dogs prefer less time working with clients	very low in home high in facilty	very low in home high in facilty	high	at home: always "at work", home/work boundaries blurred at home: can work at off hours at facility: overnight care required	can be lucrative but also stressful due to lack of down time can be a quicker approach for training results

Service	Best Suited For:	Best suited for clients who:	Relative client cost	Best suited for dog pros who:	Relative start up costs	Relative ongoing costs:	Relative revenue potential *	Impact on time	Other Notes
Group Classes	basic obedience manners puppies some dog-dog re-activity tricks, sports, specialty classes	have time and desire to actively work with their dogs	less ex-pensive	have strong teaching and coaching skills have strong organization-al skills	low to high de-pending on space costs	low to high de-pending on space costs	low to moderate depend-ing on number of classes	work is mostly nights and weekends	great way to im-pact multiple dogs and people at once can be a good marketing op-portunity for other services

Service	Best Suited For:	Best suited for clients who:	Relative client cost	Best suited for dog pros who:	Relative start up costs	Relative ongoing costs:	Relative revenue potential *	Impact on time	Other Notes
Off Leash Group Walks	social, active dogs dogs who require higher level of exercise	are unable to get dogs out due to work or infirmity have a steady income	ongoing	have strong dog skills, ability to read dog body language enjoy being outdoors and exercising are calm and able to handle the unexpected	very low unless purchasing a vehicle	low to medium depending on gas usage	moderate	work is all done during the day time used very efficiently	time spent outside generally makes up for time in car bad weather can be difficult

Service	Best Suited For:	Best suited for clients who:	Relative client cost	Best suited for dog pros who:	Relative start up costs	Relative ongoing costs:	Relative revenue potential *	Impact on time	Other Notes
On Leash Individual Walks	older dogs asocial dogs dogs with fear or aggression issues	work long hours have a steady income	ongoing	prefer less challenge and risk than group walks enjoy working with dogs one on one	very low	very low	low	can be relatively inefficient time to revenue ratio	lots of time spent in car scheduling can be tricky
On Leash Group Walks	very well socialized dogs very leash savvy dogs	work long hours have a steady income	ongoing	have an excellent sense of humor have strong leash handling skills do not have access to off leash areas	very low	very low	low to moderate	can be an efficient use of time	multiple leashed dogs can be difficult to manage

Service	Best Suited For:	Best suited for clients who:	Relative client cost	Best suited for dog pros who:	Relative start up costs	Relative ongoing costs:	Relative revenue potential *	Impact on time	Other Notes
Boarding in Your Home	social dogs if you have your own dogs dogs with special needs	want to know their dog is receiving home style care	more expensive	enjoy the company of extra dogs in their home	very low	very low	high	work/home boundaries blurred can work on own schedule	can be lucrative but also stressful due to lack of down time
House Sitting	dogs with special needs asocial dogs	want their dog in its own environment want their house looked after	expensive	enjoy working in others' homes enjoy working with a variety of animals	very low	very low	moderate	potential for working during the day	time spent away from home can lead to burnout not conducive for home relationships and having ones own pets

113

Service	Best Suited For:	Best suited for clients who:	Relative client cost	Best suited for dog pros who:	Relative start up costs	Relative ongoing costs:	Relative revenue potential *	Impact on time	Other Notes
Drop In Sitting	dogs who can tolerate long hours alone	need short term services are on a budget	less expensive	enjoy working with a variety of animals	very low	moderate due to gas usage	low to moderate	can be relatively inefficient time to revenue ration lots of night, early morning, and weekend work	lots of time spent in car

Service	Best Suited For:	Best suited for clients who:	Relative client cost	Best suited for dog pros who:	Relative start up costs	Relative ongoing costs:	Relative revenue potential *	Impact on time	Other Notes
Daycare	very social dogs with no serious behavior issues	work long hours have a steady income	ongoing	have strong dog skills, ability to read dog body language enjoy the company of groups of dogs	high	high	moderate to high	must be at facility long days M-F	some find daycare fascinating, others become bored and miss human company

Service	Best Suited For:	Best suited for clients who:	Relative client cost	Best suited for dog pros who:	Relative start up costs	Relative ongoing costs:	Relative revenue potential *	Impact on time	Other Notes
Facility Boarding	social dogs dogs with no serious behavior issues are preferable	do not want dog left in home while they are away want to keep cost relatively low	less expensive to expensive	enjoy daily ongoing company of dogs	high	high	moderate to high	conscientious boarding requires 24 hour attendance	round the clock working can lead to burnout

NOTE: Revenue potential is relative to other services on the chart, and to relative time to revenue ratio (time needed to generate the revenue), and based on a single person business. For example, one person walking two groups of dogs off leash can make a moderate income. Hiring additional people to walk for them could result in a high or even very high income.

6. ROI (Return on Investment) Tracking Sheet

Use something similar to this sheet to track how people heard about you, and the outcome of the contact. This will give you data to use when determining where to put additional marketing resources.

Date	Name	How Heard	They Their Needs	Outcome	Outcome Date	Notes
4/10/07	Barbara Polino	newsletter in Best Care Vet's office	Yorkie is resource guarding	hired for 8 session training package	4/18/07	
4/11/07	Ted Mackey	SPCA referral	8 mos old not coming when called	enrolled in adolescent manners class	4/11/07	Took adult basic class afterward

Acknowledgements

Thank you first to my editor, Rikke Jorgensen, for your tremendous improvements to this work, your straightforward advice, and your invaluable support. Thank you Gina Phairas for your insights and willingness to read and talk about whatever I put in front of you, whenever I put it there. Thank you to all those I've worked closely with and learned from at the San Francisco SPCA.

On a personal note, I thank my husband Patrick for making sure I remembered to eat—and that there was something to eat—while I was writing. And I thank my parents, Ken and Mary, for supporting everything I've ever chosen to do.

Author Biography

Veronica Boutelle, MA, CTC, is the former Director of Behavior and Training at the San Francisco SPCA. Through her business, dogTEC, she teaches sold-out seminars and consults one-on-one with dog professionals. Veronica writes the column "The Business End of the Leash" for the APDT Chronicle of the Dog and is a sought-after speaker at conferences and dog training schools across the country. She lives with her husband, two dogs, surrounded by wildlife in Sixes, Oregon.

INDEX

A

Accountant, 9, 91
     tax, 18
Active marketing, 30-32
Administrative tasks, vii
Advice, avoiding giving free, 81-86
Aggression cases, 56
Assistants, 73
Association of Pet Dog Trainers (APDT), 2, 5, 16, 95
Assumed business name (ABN), 11
Attorney, 9, 15
Audience, know your, 26

B

Behavior modification, 2, 44, 50, 51-52
Benefits, emphasizing, 25-26
Board and train, 46
Boarding, 48
Body language, 2
Bookkeeper, 9, 91
Books, 4, 94-95
Boss, being your own, v-vi
Budgeting, 6-7, 97-100
Burnout, 56, 74-87
Business expansion, 66-68
Business license, 10-11, 20, 101
Business names, 24
Buzzwords, 3

C

Cancellation policies, 55
Chat groups, 3
Clicker Solutions list, 3
Clients
    keeping contact information on, 8
    marketing to, 24-25
    setting expectations of, 77-81
    who you want them to be, 26
Coach, 9
Competition, 23
Continuing education, 5, 93-94

Contracts, 15-16, 20
Corporation, 18
Creativity, 28

D
Daycare operators, vii, 84, 95-96, 115-16
    cancellation policies of, 55-56
    follow-up for, 40-41
    liability coverage for, 16
    packaging for, 49
    service-related issues, 48
    start-up capital for, 7
    training for, 3
    volunteer, 1
Day training, 45-46
Deadlines, 37
Discounts, 50-51
Dog runs, 23
DogTEC, 92
Dog TEC Dog Walking Academy, 3
Dogwise, 5
Doing business as certificate (DBA), 11
Dunbar, Ian, 2

E
Efficiency, 64-66
Employees, 68-69, 90
Environment, consider your, 27
Expectations, setting client, 77-81

F
Families, working with , 23
Fear of failure, 37
Federal Employer Identification Number (FEIN), 13-14, 20, 102
Fictitious business name (FBN), 11-12, 20, 102
Follow-up, 39-41
Full time, transitioning to, 60-64

G
Generalist, 23
Groomers, vii
Group classes, 46-47

H
Home, running business from, 11

I
Independent contractor, 7, 69-71, 80
In-home training, 44-45
Insurance, 16-17, 20, 90, 103
Insurance agent, 9
International Association of Animal Behavior Consultants (IAABC), 5, 95
Interns, 73

L
Lawsuit, 14
Legal requirements, 10-14
Liability risk, 2, 14-19, 84
Limited liability companies (LLC), 17-19, 20, 101

M
Marketing, vii, 27-38, 91-92, 104
    active, 30-32
    finding your message, 22-27
    in waves, 89
    six month rule, 88
    tracking success of, 37-38
Mentor, 4

N
National Association of Professional Pet Sitters (NAPPS), 3, 96
Newsletter, 3
Niche, finding your, 22-24

O
Online courses, 3

P
Packaging, 48-53
Partnership, 17, 71-73
Parttime, 60-64
Payment policies, 57
Peacable Paws, 3
Personality, your, v-vi
Petsitters, vii, 84, 96, 113-14
    assistants for, 73
    cancellation policies for, 56
    follow-up for, 40-41
    liability coverage for, 16
    service-related issues for, 47-48
    start-up capital for, 7
    training for, 3
    volunteer, 1

Pet Sitters International (PSI), 3, 16, 96
Phone, setting boundaries for, 76-77
Phone book ads, 31-32
Policies, 55-59, 105
Print advertising, 31
Problem solve, ability to, vi
Pro bono work, 86
Professional organizations, 9, 102. *See also* APDT, DogTEC, IAABC, NAPPS, PSI.

R
Rates, 53-55, 105
     changing, 58
Recommendations, 27, 28, 30
Referrals, 36, 41-42
Relationships, creating, 29-30
Return on investment (ROI), marketing, 37-38, 117
Right to sue, 16
Risks
     assessing, 6, 19
     comfort level with, 19
     taking, vi
Routine, lack of, 74-76

S
School, 2-4, 93
Self-assessment, vi
Self-discipline, vi
Self-employment taxes, 62
Seminars, 5
Service comparison chart, 107-16
Service mark, 12-13, 20, 90, 103
Shelter
     recommendations from, 28, 30
     volunteer at, 1
Sole proprietor, 17
Start-up capital, 7
Start-up to-do list, 101-03
Strengths, consider your, 27
Systems, 7-8

T
1099 form, 69
Tawzer Dog Videos, 5
Trainer certification, 2
Trainers, vii, 93-95, 107-10
     assistants, 73

avoiding free advice, 82-84
cancellation policies, 55
and clients, 79, 80
follow-up for, 39-41
homework compliance for, 56
liability coverage for, 16
packaging, 48-49, 51-52
school for, 2-4
service-related issues of, 43-47
start-up capital for, 7
volunteer, 1

U
URL, 13

V
Veterinary clinics, vii
Volunteer, 1, 86

W
Walkers, vii, 76, 84, 95-96, 111-12
assistants for, 73
cancellation policies of, 55-56
and clients, 79
follow-up for, 40-41
liability coverage for, 16
packaging, 49
service-related issues of, 47
start-up capital for, 7
training for, 3
volunteering, 1
Waiver, 15
Website, 13, 33-34, 94
Word of mouth, 27

Z
Zoning exemption, 11

BEHAVIOR & TRAINING

ABC's of Behavior Shaping; Fundamentals of Training; Proactive Behavior Mgmt, DVD. Ted Turner

Aggression In Dogs: Practical Mgmt, Prevention & Behaviour Modification. Brenda Aloff

Am I Safe? DVD. Sarah Kalnajs

Behavior Problems in Dogs, 3rd ed. William Campbell

Brenda Aloff's Fundamentals: Foundation Training for Every Dog, DVD. Brenda Aloff

Bringing Light to Shadow. A Dog Trainer's Diary. Pam Dennison

Canine Body Language. A Photographic Guide to the Native Language of Dogs. Brenda Aloff

Clicked Retriever. Lana Mitchell

Dog Behavior Problems: The Counselor's Handbook. William Campbell

Dog Friendly Gardens, Garden Friendly Dogs. Cheryl Smith

Dog Language, An Encyclopedia of Canine Behavior. Roger Abrantes

Evolution of Canine Social Behavior, 2nd ed. Roger Abrantes

Give Them a Scalpel and They Will Dissect a Kiss, DVD. Ian Dunbar

Guide To Professional Dog Walking And Home Boarding. Dianne Eibner

Language of Dogs, DVD. Sarah Kalnajs

Mastering Variable Surface Tracking, Component Tracking (2 bk set). Ed Presnall

My Dog Pulls. What Do I Do? Turid Rugaas

New Knowledge of Dog Behavior (reprint). Clarence Pfaffenberger

On Talking Terms with Dogs: Calming Signals, 2nd edition. Turid Rugaas

On Talking Terms with Dogs: What Your Dog Tells You, DVD. Turid Rugaas

Positive Perspectives: Love Your Dog, Train Your Dog. Pat Miller

Predation and Family Dogs, DVD. Jean Donaldson

Really Reliable Recall. Train Your Dog to Come When Called, DVD. Leslie Nelson

Right on Target. Taking Dog Training to a New Level. Mandy Book & Cheryl Smith

Stress in Dogs. Martina Scholz & Clarissa von Reinhardt

The Dog Trainer's Resource: The APDT Chronicle of the Dog Collection. Mychelle Blake (*ed*)

Therapy Dogs: Training Your Dog To Reach Others. Kathy Diamond Davis

Training Dogs, A Manual (reprint). Konrad Most

Training the Disaster Search Dog. Shirley Hammond

Try Tracking: The Puppy Tracking Primer. Carolyn Krause
Visiting the Dog Park, Having Fun, and Staying Safe. Cheryl S. Smith
When Pigs Fly. Train Your Impossible Dog. Jane Killion
Winning Team. A Guidebook for Junior Showmanship. Gail Haynes
Working Dogs (reprint). Elliot Humphrey & Lucien Warner

HEALTH & ANATOMY, SHOWING
An Eye for a Dog. Illustrated Guide to Judging Purebred Dogs. Robert Cole
Annie On Dogs! Ann Rogers Clark
Canine Cineradiography DVD. Rachel Page Elliott
Canine Massage: A Complete Reference Manual.
Jean-Pierre Hourdebaigt
Canine Terminology (reprint). Harold Spira
Dog In Action (reprint). Macdowell Lyon
Dogsteps DVD. Rachel Page Elliott
Performance Dog Nutrition: Optimize Performance With Nutrition.
Jocelynn Jacobs
Positive Training for Show Dogs: Building a Relationship for Success
Vicki Ronchette
Puppy Intensive Care: A Breeder's Guide To Care Of Newborn Puppies. Myra
Savant Harris
Raw Dog Food: Make It Easy for You and Your Dog. Carina MacDonald
Raw Meaty Bones. Tom Lonsdale
Shock to the System. The Facts About Animal Vaccination...
Catherine O'Driscoll
The History and Management of the Mastiff. Elizabeth Baxter & Pat Hoffman
Work Wonders. Feed Your Dog Raw Meaty Bones. Tom Lonsdale
Whelping Healthy Puppies, DVD. Sylvia Smart

Dogwise.com is your complete source for dog books on the web!

2,000+ titles, fast shipping, and excellent customer service.

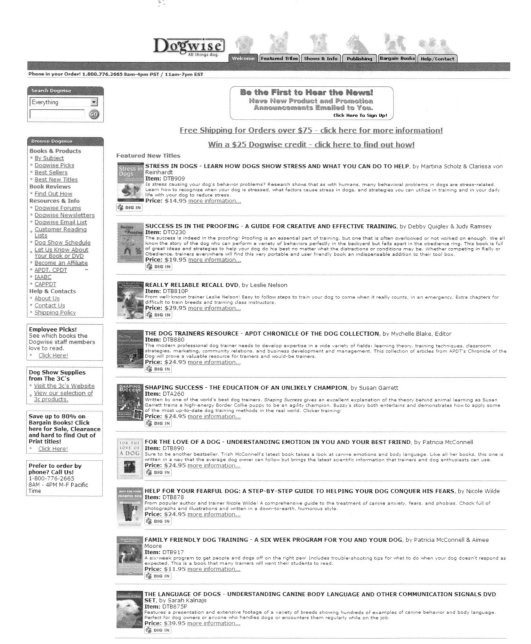

Dogwise All things dog.

Welcome | Featured Titles | Shows & Info | Publishing | Bargain Books | Help/Contact

Phone in your Order! 1.800.776.2665 8am-4pm PST / 11am-7pm EST

Search Dogwise
Everything

Browse Dogwise

Books & Products
* By Subject
* Dogwise Picks
* Best Sellers
* Best New Titles

Book Reviews
* Find Out How

Resources & Info
* Dogwise Forums
* Dogwise Newsletters
* Dogwise Email List
* Customer Reading Lists
* Dog Show Schedule
* Let Us Know About Your Book or DVD
* Become an Affiliate
* APDT, CPDT
* IAABC
* CAPPDT

Help & Contacts
* About Us
* Contact Us
* Shipping Policy

Employee Picks!
See which books the Dogwise staff members love to read.
* Click Here!

Dog Show Supplies from The 3C's
* Visit the 3c's Website
* View our selection of 3c products.

Save up to 80% on Bargain Books! Click here for Sale, Clearance and hard to find Out of Print titles!
* Click Here!

Prefer to order by phone? Call Us!
1-800-776-2665
8AM - 4PM M-F Pacific Time

Featured New Titles

STRESS IN DOGS - LEARN HOW DOGS SHOW STRESS AND WHAT YOU CAN DO TO HELP, by Martina Scholz & Clarissa von Reinhardt
Item: DTB909
Is stress causing your dog's behavior problems? Research shows that as with humans, many behavioral problems in dogs are stress-related. Learn how to recognize when your dog is stressed, what factors cause stress in dogs, and strategies you can utilize in training and in your daily life with your dog to reduce stress.
Price: $14.95 more information...
DIG IN

SUCCESS IS IN THE PROOFING - A GUIDE FOR CREATIVE AND EFFECTIVE TRAINING, by Debby Quigley & Judy Ramsey
Item: DTO230
The success is indeed in the proofing! Proofing is an essential part of training, but one that is often overlooked or not worked on enough. We all know the story of the dog who can perform a variety of behaviors perfectly in the backyard but falls apart in the obedience ring. This book is full of great ideas and strategies to help your dog do his best no matter what the distractions or conditions may be. Whether competing in Rally or Obedience, trainers everywhere will find this very portable and user friendly book an indispensable addition to their tool box.
Price: $19.95 more information...
DIG IN

REALLY RELIABLE RECALL DVD, by Leslie Nelson
Item: DTB810P
From well-known trainer Leslie Nelson! Easy to follow steps to train your dog to come when it really counts, in an emergency. Extra chapters for difficult to train breeds and training class instructors.
Price: $29.95 more information...
DIG IN

THE DOG TRAINERS RESOURCE - APDT CHRONICLE OF THE DOG COLLECTION, by Mychelle Blake, Editor
Item: DTB880
The modern professional dog trainer needs to develop expertise in a wide variety of fields: learning theory, training techniques, classroom strategies, marketing, community relations, and business development and management. This collection of articles from APDT's Chronicle of the Dog will prove a valuable resource for trainers and would-be trainers.
Price: $24.95 more information...
DIG IN

SHAPING SUCCESS - THE EDUCATION OF AN UNLIKELY CHAMPION, by Susan Garrett
Item: DTA260
Written by one of the world's best dog trainers, Shaping Success gives an excellent explanation of the theory behind animal learning as Susan Garrett trains a high-energy Border Collie puppy to be an agility champion. Buzzy's story both entertains and demonstrates how to apply some of the most up-to-date dog training methods in the real world. Clicker training!
Price: $24.95 more information...
DIG IN

FOR THE LOVE OF A DOG - UNDERSTANDING EMOTION IN YOU AND YOUR BEST FRIEND, by Patricia McConnell
Item: DTB890
Sure to be another bestseller, Trish McConnell's latest book takes a look at canine emotions and body language. Like all her books, this one is written in a way that the average dog owner can follow but brings the latest scientific information that trainers and dog enthusiasts can use.
Price: $24.95 more information...
DIG IN

HELP FOR YOUR FEARFUL DOG: A STEP-BY-STEP GUIDE TO HELPING YOUR DOG CONQUER HIS FEARS, by Nicole Wilde
Item: DTB878
From popular author and trainer Nicole Wilde! A comprehensive guide to the treatment of canine anxiety, fears, and phobias. Chock full of photographs and illustrations and written in a down-to-earth, humorous style.
Price: $24.95 more information...
DIG IN

FAMILY FRIENDLY DOG TRAINING - A SIX WEEK PROGRAM FOR YOU AND YOUR DOG, by Patricia McConnell & Aimee Moore
Item: DTB917
A six-week program to get people and dogs off on the right paw! Includes trouble-shooting tips for what to do when your dog doesn't respond as expected. This is a book that many trainers will want their students to read.
Price: $11.95 more information...
DIG IN

THE LANGUAGE OF DOGS - UNDERSTANDING CANINE BODY LANGUAGE AND OTHER COMMUNICATION SIGNALS DVD SET, by Sarah Kalnajs
Item: DTB875P
Features a presentation and extensive footage of a variety of breeds showing hundreds of examples of canine behavior and body language. Perfect for dog owners or anyone who handles dogs or encounters them regularly while on the job.
Price: $39.95 more information...
DIG IN